MYP by Concept

Language & Literature

Ana de Castro
Zara Kaiserimam
Series editor: Paul Morris

Boost

HODDER
EDUCATION
AN HACHETTE UK COMPANY

Authors' dedication

For Zara, for her generosity of spirit and wonderful creativity.
Ana
To my mother for her encouragement and unwavering support.
Zara

Hachette UK's policy is to use papers that are natural, renewable and recyclable products and made from wood grown in well-managed forests and other controlled sources. The logging and manufacturing processes are expected to conform to the environmental regulations of the country of origin.

Orders: please contact Hachette UK Distribution, Hely Hutchinson Centre, Milton Road, Didcot, Oxfordshire, OX11 7HH. Telephone: +44 (0)1235 827827. Email education@hachette.co.uk Lines are open from 9 a.m. to 5 p.m., Monday to Friday. You can also order through our website: www.hoddereducation.com

Published by Hodder Education
An Hachette UK Company
Carmelite House, 50 Victoria Embankment, London EC4Y 0DZ

Impression number   11
Year   2024

Cover photo © nevarpp/123RF.com

Illustrations by DC Graphic Design Limited
Typeset in Frutiger LT Std 45 Light 10/14pt by DC Graphic Design Limited, Hextable, Kent
Printed in Great Britian by Bell and Bain Ltd, Glasgow

A catalogue record for this title is available from the British Library

ISBN 9781471880735

Contents

How to use this book

Welcome to Hodder Education's *MYP by Concept* series! Each chapter is designed to lead you through an *inquiry* into the concepts of Language and literature, and how they interact in real-life global contexts.

The *Statement of Inquiry* provides the framework for this inquiry, and the *Inquiry questions* then lead us through the exploration as they are developed through each chapter.

Each chapter is framed with a *Key concept* and a *Related concept* and is set in a *Global context*.

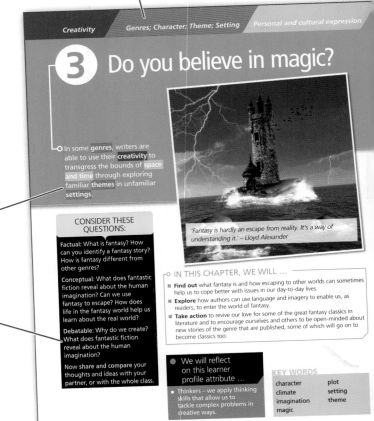

KEY WORDS

Key words are included to give you access to vocabulary for the topic. **Glossary terms** are highlighted and, where applicable, **search terms** are given to encourage independent learning and research skills.

As you explore, activities suggest ways to learn through *action*.

ATL

Activities are designed to develop your *Approaches to Learning* (ATL) skills.

EXTENSION

Extension activities allow you to explore a topic further.

◆ Assessment opportunities in this chapter:

Some activities are *formative* as they allow you to practise certain of the MYP Language and literature *Assessment Objectives*. Other activities can be used by you or your teachers to assess your achievement against all parts of an Assessment Objective.

Key *Approaches to Learning* skills for MYP Language and literature are highlighted whenever we encounter them.

Hint

In some of the Activities, we provide Hints to help you work on the assignment. This also introduces you to the new Hint feature in the on-screen assessment.

ⓘ Definitions are included for important terms and information boxes are included to give background information, more detail and explanation.

You are prompted to consider your conceptual understanding in a variety of activities throughout each chapter.

We have incorporated Visible Thinking – ideas, framework, protocol and thinking routines – from Project Zero at the Harvard Graduate School of Education into many of our activities.

At the end of the chapter you are asked to reflect on what you have learnt with our *Reflection table*, maybe to think of new questions brought to light by your learning.

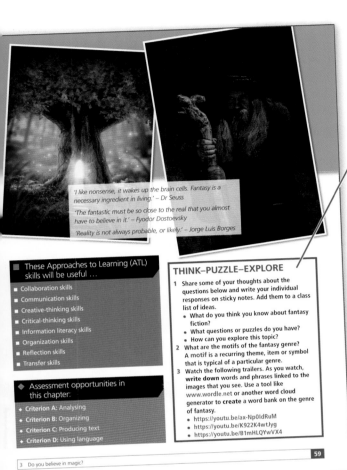

'I like nonsense, it wakes up the brain cells. Fantasy is a necessary ingredient in living.' – Dr Seuss

'The fantastic must be so close to the real that you almost have to believe in it.' – Fyodor Dostoevsky

'Reality is not always probable, or likely.' – Jorge Luis Borges

These Approaches to Learning (ATL) skills will be useful …

- Collaboration skills
- Communication skills
- Creative-thinking skills
- Critical-thinking skills
- Information literacy skills
- Organization skills
- Reflection skills
- Transfer skills

◆ Assessment opportunities in this chapter:

- ◆ Criterion A: Analysing
- ◆ Criterion B: Organizing
- ◆ Criterion C: Producing text
- ◆ Criterion D: Using language

THINK–PUZZLE–EXPLORE

1 Share some of your thoughts about the questions below and write your individual responses on sticky notes. Add them to a class list of ideas.
- What do you think you know about fantasy fiction?
- What questions or puzzles do you have?
- How can you explore this topic?
2 What are the motifs of the fantasy genre? A motif is a recurring theme, item or symbol that is typical of a particular genre.
3 Watch the following trailers. As you watch, **write down** words and phrases linked to the images that you see. Use a tool like www.wordle.net or another word cloud generator to **create** a word bank on the genre of fantasy.
- https://youtu.be/ax-Np0IdRuM
- https://youtu.be/K922K4wtJyg
- https://youtu.be/B1mHLQYwVX4

59

3   Do you believe in magic?

Use this table to reflect on your own learning in this chapter.					
Questions we asked	Answers we found	Any further questions now?			
Factual					
Conceptual					
Debatable					
Approaches to learning you used in this chapter:	Description – what new skills did you learn?	How well did you master the skills?			
		Novice	Learner	Practitioner	Expert
Learner profile attribute(s)	*Reflect on the importance of the attribute for your learning in this chapter.*				

! Take action

! While the book provides many opportunities for action and plenty of content to enrich the conceptual relationships, you must be an active part of this process. Guidance is given to help you with your own research, including how to carry out research, how to form your own research questions, and how to link and develop your study of Language and literature to the global issues in our twenty-first-century world.

● We will reflect on this learner profile attribute …

● Each chapter has a *IB learner profile* attribute as its theme, and you are encouraged to reflect on these too.

▼ Links to:

Like any other subject, Language and literature is just one part of our bigger picture of the world. Links to other subjects are discussed.

1 Is seeing always believing?

○ Through **communication** directors **create film** to **position** audiences to **respond** in a particular way.

CONSIDER THESE QUESTIONS:

Factual: What is a documentary? What are the conventions of a documentary? How did documentary filmmaking get started? What types of documentary are there? What different TV genres are there?

Conceptual: How real is the reality in a documentary? How do documentary films differ from other types of films? Is language changing in film and television? What conventions are used to communicate with an audience in the genre of documentary?

Debatable: Are ethical issues central to documentary filmmaking?

Now **share** and **compare** your thoughts and ideas with your partner, or with the whole class.

Doing a documentary is about discovering, being open, learning and following curiosity.

■ Award-winning filmmaker, Spike Jonze

○ IN THIS CHAPTER, WE WILL ...

■ **Find out** how documentaries can expand our awareness of the world around us.

■ **Explore** current viewing trends and the effectiveness of media to lead to change.

■ **Take action** by working on projects that make a real and positive difference; by striving to tell community stories of importance; by not being scared of a challenge and by always asking why.

These Approaches to Learning (ATL) skills will be useful …

- Collaboration skills
- Communication skills
- Creative-thinking skills
- Critical-thinking skills
- Information literacy skills
- Media literacy skills
- Reflection skills

We will reflect on this learner profile attribute …

- Open-minded – we understand and embrace other cultures. We recognize and celebrate our own backgrounds and learn tolerance for others.

Assessment opportunities in this chapter:

- **Criterion A:** Analysing
- **Criterion B:** Organizing
- **Criterion C:** Producing text
- **Criterion D:** Using language

KEY WORDS

accuracy	footage
broadcast	non-fiction
documentarian	objective
documentary	subjective
fiction	watershed

ACTIVITY: Question starts

ATL

- Collaboration skills: Listen actively to other perspectives and ideas

1. In pairs, **discuss** what makes a good question. How can asking good questions help you find out more about a topic?
2. Question starts are part of a routine that can help you brainstorm, provoke thinking and inquire into a topic. Let's look at the question starts below.

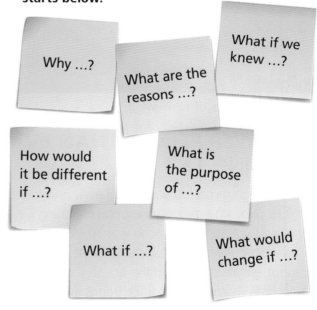

3. In pairs, brainstorm at least twelve questions about TV genres and programmes. Write your questions on sticky notes.
4. Review the brainstormed list and put an asterisk by the questions that seem most interesting. Then select one or more of these questions to **discuss** for a few moments.
5. Reflect: What new ideas do you have about the topic, concept or object that you didn't have before?

What different TV genres are there?

■ The changing face of TV viewing

ARE FEWER PEOPLE THAN EVER WATCHING TV?

What TV programmes do you, your family and friends watch? How much time do you spend watching TV and how do you decide what to watch? How do your viewing preferences shape your ideas, how you feel about certain things and the action you take? These questions are used to track trends and explore the choices we make about how to spend our free time and the viewing experiences we prefer. They are indicators that highlight how our society is changing and how the media adapts to those changes.

Recent studies indicate that a growing number of households are no longer watching TV and that it is only a matter of time before we see the total disappearance of TV as we know it. Social media, streaming services and the amount of time we spend surfing the web affect not only how we communicate

but also how we spend our free time. It is perhaps surprising therefore that Nielsen, a firm that tracks trends, has found that TV is still by far America's favourite entertainment pastime.

In this chapter, we will consider current viewing trends and take a close look at the documentary genre. By analysing the documentary *Sounds Like Teen Spirit*, we will **comment** on the **purpose** of documentaries, **critique** the text through active viewing and **examine** critical issues that affect the lives of children today.

ACTIVITY: Genres

■ ATL

■ Media literacy skills: Make informed choices about personal viewing experiences

Individually, **list** the different types of programmes you watch and/or those broadcast in your country. In pairs, **compare** your lists and group them into programme types. Visit the link below and look at the genres listed. Create a table to **classify** your programmes under each genre: **www.bbc.co.uk/programmes/genres**.

Share information with your classmates and **discuss** any differences in points of view.

Are there any TV genres under which you have not listed a programme?

Visit the links below and **explore** the programmes from the online TV guides to complete your table:
- **www.freeview.co.uk/tv-guide**
- **www.radiotimes.com/tv/tv-listings**
- **http://tv.sky.com/tv-guide**.

Compare and contrast the TV guides in your country with the ones above. In pairs, **compare and contrast** the differences and similarities. **Evaluate** the quality of programmes on offer. Who decides what programmes are broadcast in your country? Are all the channels free?

◆ Assessment opportunities

◆ In this activity you have practised skills that are assessed using Criterion A: Analysing.

ACTIVITY: Finding facts

ATL

- Communication skills: Preview and skim texts to build understanding; read critically and for comprehension

Finding the facts in a reading text requires practice. Read the article, 'Why people watch television': https://bit.ly/39QYHgD

1 As you read, pick out any points about why people watch television. Copy and complete the table below, adding any evidence you have found.

A study from Thinkbox suggests ...	
Research from YouView suggests ...	
Six reasons why people watch TV are ...	
Broadcasters see their purpose as ...	

2 Read the article again and write out the part of the text that tells you about the following:
   a the differences between live TV and the on-demand experience
   b what some programme makers may find disappointing
   c facts that show what people watch in a week
   d programmes that are 'live' and figures linked to live viewing
   e programmes that are 'recorded' and data linked to recorded viewing
   f habits of viewers
   g reliability of surveys
   h what else is needed, according to the writer.

◆ Assessment opportunities

- In this activity you have practised skills that are assessed using Criterion A: Analysing.

▼ Links to: Sciences

■ C. Lorenz company TV set from the 1950s

Did you know that it was the inventions and discoveries of many different scientists that resulted in giving us television?

The 'first' generation of television sets were very different from what we have now and were not entirely electronic. The TV screen had a small motor with a spinning disc and a neon lamp, which worked together to give a blurry reddish-orange image about five centimetres wide. The period before 1935 is called the 'Mechanical Television Era'.

Visit this website: https://bit.ly/3oHssG4 and research the scientists who invented the television.

▼ Links to: History

The first experiments with television broadcasting were conducted in the 1920s and 1930s in Great Britain and the United States. In 1936 the British Broadcasting Corporation (BBC) started the world's first television broadcast and in America the first programme was broadcast in 1941.

- Use a search engine, such as Google, to carry out your research. Why not try Google Knowledge Graph to narrow down your search. Another useful tool is instaGrok, a search engine that generates a web of related videos, images articles, and terms based on a specific query. You can also use instaGrok to evaluate sources.

- Create a timeline representing the evolution of TV and TV broadcasting in your country. To get you started go to: www.tvhistory.tv/index.html.

ACTIVITY: Writing sentences

■ ATL

■ Critical-thinking skills: Practise observing carefully in order to recognize problems

Sentences are necessary to written communication. There really is no better way to share your point of view other than with a fantastically well-written sentence. Learning how to use language correctly and identifying parts of a sentence will help you to do this.

Task 1

In pairs, **identify** why each of the following is not an accurate sentence:

1 **The boy pushed his bike slowly into the garage, upset by the damage the car had caused.**
2 **Apples for £1.99 a kilo.**
3 **Rode home.**
4 **Valeria told that she liked San José.**
5 **He wants to go but his mother won't agree.**
6 **After the summer.**
7 **The sun on my face.**
8 **Walked up the hill.**

> **Hint**
> A verb is a word used for a state of 'being' or 'doing' an action.

Task 2

In pairs, **identify** each of the following as a phrase, clause or main clause:

1 **running to the sea**
2 **Álvaro sighed, exasperated**
3 **on the way to the tube**
4 **they went to the Rolling Stones concert**

5 **despite the heavy traffic**
6 **in the summer**
7 **the Grand Canyon is impressive**
8 **The scorpion's deadly sting**
9 **Nathan sneezed**
10 **Joseph talks in his sleep.**

Task 3

In pairs or groups of three, look at the notes you made on the text, 'Why people watch television' (Activity: Finding facts). Write your own sentences about why people watch television.

Use some of the phrases in the box to make your sentences more interesting.

For me. …	As far as I'm concerned, …
In my view …	
In my opinion, …	My own feeling on the subject is that …
If you ask me, …	I would say that …
To my mind, …	It seems to me …
To my way of thinking, I'd say …	I am of the opinion …
I've come to the conclusion …	My impression is …

◆ Assessment opportunities

◆ In this activity you have practised skills that are assessed using Criterion C: Producing text and Criterion D: Using language.

Understanding sentences

• A sentence in English must include a verb.
• A phrase is a group of words without a verb.
• A clause is a group of words with a verb.
• A main clause is a clause which has meaning on its own and could be a sentence.

■ The first national TV Guide was launched in the USA in 1953. The prototype (the first version) of *TV Guide* magazine was developed by Lee Wagner (1910–1993), and there were early examples of regional TV guides as early as the 1930s

ACTIVITY: How television works

There is no doubt that TV is one of the most influential innovations of our time. But have you ever wondered how it works? What's the technology behind a TV? How can hundreds of channels of complete images arrive at your house? How do televisions decode the signals to produce the image? How will digital television change our viewing experiences?

- **In groups of three, research** how television works. **Summarize the information and create a PowerPoint presentation for your classmates. Don't forget to predict what the future holds for TV.**
- **How has TV evolved? Have you seen images of the first television sets? What do the latest television models on the market look like?**
- **Watch this short clip of the evolution of television over 100 years:**
  https://youtu.be/J8R4ZoIMx7M.
- **As you watch …**
  - **Make notes on the design, materials used, size, shape and any other element you think is important about the design of TV sets.**
  - **Consider the factors that have influenced the design and evolution of TV sets.**
  - **In pairs, use your notes to create an infographic to show the evolution of design and technology in television.**
  - **In groups of three, design the television of the future, what it will look like and what it will be able to do. Justify your choice of design.**

Infographics

A well-designed infographic, like the example below, can help you simplify a complicated subject and represent information visually to grab the attention of your audience.

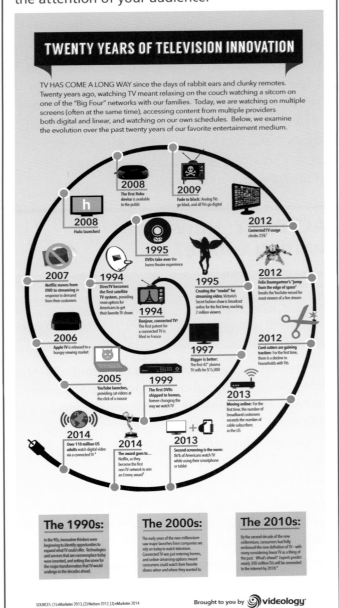

TWENTY YEARS OF TELEVISION INNOVATION

TV HAS COME A LONG WAY since the days of rabbit ears and clunky remotes. Twenty years ago, watching TV meant relaxing on the couch watching a sitcom on one of the "Big Four" networks with our families. Today, we are watching on multiple screens (often at the same time), accessing content from multiple providers both digital and linear, and watching on our own schedules. Below, we examine the evolution over the past twenty years of our favorite entertainment medium.

■ Twenty years of television innovation

Adding interactive content such as infographics to your presentations can help the audience to engage with the topic, and makes information not only more accessible but also memorable.

Is language changing in film and television?

We do not remember learning how to speak, but learning to write is an ongoing process that involves learning to use language correctly and practising in order to become a good writer. In fact, humans were able to speak one hundred thousand years ago, but it was not until much later that we felt the need to represent sounds graphically in order to keep them, and thus writing was born.

ACTIVITY: How did writing evolve?

■ ATL

- Information literacy skills: Collect, record and verify data

Written language is not always represented in the same way. Find out about the following writing systems and **summarize** the information you find on:
- pictographic writing
- alphabetic writing
- ideographic script.

You could speak to students in your class who use different alphabetical systems or ideographic languages.

◆ Assessment opportunities

- ◆ In this activity you have practised skills that are assessed using Criterion C: Producing text and Criterion D: Using language.

Register is an important feature of both spoken and written language. It refers to the **tone**, style, word choice and degree of formality of language. Whether speaking or writing, it is essential to use the register that is most appropriate to your audience and purpose.

Standard English is appropriate to all formal situations, as well as many informal situations. At other times, you need to consider the purpose of the text, the audience and the effect you want to achieve in writing or speaking.

Oral and written language are two different systems that we use in various communication processes.

- Oral communication includes conversations, television debates, TV and radio interviews.
- Written communication includes letters, novels and newspaper articles.

Standard English

Standard English is the style of English language (grammar, vocabulary and spelling) that is widely accepted in spoken and written form. Standard English is used to communicate in formal and some informal contexts. It is considered the appropriate choice of style in media writing and TV and radio news announcements.

Colloquial language is informal language, and there may be variations in words or phrases used that are specific to a geographical area or region.

Slang is very informal language. It is creative language, and it is usually linked to the world of music and fashion. Slang is related to the language young people use, and every generation creates their own slang words and phrases. It's tough to keep up with the latest modern words!

Use a search engine to find out about the different styles of language and write down some examples for each style. How does register affect each style?

Received Pronunciation and BBC English

Is there such a thing as BBC English? What is Received Pronunciation?

The BBC is the British Broadcasting Corporation, the world's oldest broadcasting organization. It used to be the case that presenters on the BBC spoke in a certain way. These days, broadcasters tend to speak with a broader range of accents.

Before the Second World War, in the early days of television, radio announcers and newsreaders did speak with **Received Pronunciation** or RP, as it is also known. RP was more common in the southern part of England, and it is linked to a social class rather than 'a particular type of English'. It is sometimes also referred to as the Queen's English. Search **Received Pronunciation** and listen to some old broadcasts to hear what it sounds like.

The BBC should represent the diversity of the British Isles – the variety of accents and dialects found across the United Kingdom should be reflected in the voices that are heard on programmes such as the news. But is this the case?

Watch the following clip of Scottish poet, Tom Leonard, reading his poem 'The Six O'Clock News' (1:44-2:38): **https://bit.ly/3qCdmmJ**.

THINK–PAIR–SHARE

1 **Identify** the attitudes Leonard is expressing in the poem.
2 Are you able to understand everything he says? Can you rewrite the poem using Standard English?
3 Do we make assumptions about people (their social status, level of education, intelligence, honesty) based on the way they speak?
4 What is your opinion about this? Should people be judged for the way they speak?

The Six O'Clock News

this is thi
six a clock
news thi
man said n
thi reason
a talk wia
BBC accent
iz coz yi
widny wahnt
mi ti talk
aboot thi
trooth wia
voice lik
wanna yoo
scruff. if
a toktaboot
thi trooth
lik wanna yoo
scruff yi
widny thingk

it wuz troo.
jist wanna yoo
scruff tokn.
thirza right
way ti spell
ana right way
to tok it. this
is me tokn yir
right way a
spellin. this
is ma trooth.
yooz doant no
thi trooth
yirsellz cawz
yi canny talk
right. this is
the six a clock
nyooz. belt up.

Tom Leonard

Sounds Like Teen Spirit (2008)

Sounds Like Teen Spirit (also known as Sounds Like Teen Spirit: A Popumentary) is directed by Bafta-award nominated director, Jamie Jay Johnson. The documentary is about the lives of the participants of the Junior Eurovision Song Contest in 2007. The film follows the participants as they proceed from the national finals to being crowned the representatives of their country through to the international song festival, held in Rotterdam, the Netherlands.

Read this transcript for the trailer for the documentary, Sounds Like Teen Spirit:

(UNIDENTIFIED VOICE): OK. Stand by everybody, for rehearsal. Just a minute just a minute … We've got a slight technical hitch with the audio … Stand by. Here we go.

I love flags. I don't know why, but I love flags and as soon as I see the contest starting with all those flags being waved I'm in heaven.

(IONA PRACTISES HER PRONUNCIATION)

COMMENTATOR: I think Ukraine will be the winner.

COMMENTATOR: Cyprus

COMMENTATOR: Belgium

COMMENTATOR: Is a very good group, but they are … Too old, too big?

(MUSIC)

FEMALE PRESENTER: I am nearly wetting myself with excitement!

(MUSIC – GIORGOS' SONG)

GIORGOS: When I sing you're in a different world. I could forget about all the teasing and that … They called me gay because I hated football.

(MUSIC – BON BON'S SONG)

MARINA: When I go on stage I really hope I'm gonna make my dad proud because, if he's watching, that means he cares.

(MUSIC – TRUST'S SONG)

LAURENS: I tried to dance, I make some movements – we are boys, we can't dance!

(MUSIC – DALTON SISTERS)

MALE PRESENTER: The whole Europe can see us.

CONTESTANT: Hello from Georgia!

CONTESTANT: Belarus

CONTESTANT: Russia

CONTESTANT: I am from Ukraine.

CONTESTANT: I come from Serbia.

DIRECTOR: Try to look cheerful.

(MUSIC – DALTON SISTERS)

PRIEST: Hard Rock

DIRECTOR: You like Hard Rock? Pink Floyd, Led Zeppelin?

ELIANA: I've never felt so happy in all my life.

COMMENTATOR: I wish the Macedonian team all the best and … with the help of God, we'll be … second or third.

DALTON SISTERS: Hey!

ACTIVITY: Analysing a transcript

ATL

- Critical-thinking skills: Draw reasonable conclusions and generalizations

Task 1

Individually, create a table like the one below, adding in the characteristics of spoken and written language (an example has been provided). **Compare** your list with a partner and share your ideas.

Characteristics of spoken language	Characteristics of written language
It is immediate and allows interaction between speaker and the listener.	It is deferred: the message is usually received after it has been issued.

Task 2

In groups of three, look at the transcript for the *Sounds Like Teen Spirit* trailer (see page 10) and **identify** the elements of spoken language and communication. Add new ideas to your table.

Task 3

Visit this website and complete the quiz on register and audience: **https://bit.ly/3sCtaId**.

Look back at the transcript and **identify** the register being used.

Task 4

Now watch the trailer for the film: **https://youtu.be/K0wMn3cMrnI**.

As you listen, **compare and contrast** the transcript and the trailer.

Assessment opportunities

- In this activity you have practised skills that are assessed using Criterion A: Analysing.

Oral texts

Oral texts are everywhere. We can explore the way culture and identity are reflected in our use of language and how our language changes with changes in society and technology. We can analyse spoken texts in the same way that we can analyse written texts.

The **context** of a spoken text is important as there are no genres in spoken language. To **analyse** spoken language you must consider the elements below:

Accent
The way in which words and letters are pronounced. Accent can vary according to the region or social class of the speaker.

Dialect
The grammar and vocabulary used and linked to a particular region.

Intonation
This is essential to communication and is linked to how we say things, rather than what we say. It affects the meaning we give to words and phrases.

Interruption
When someone does not wait for the speaker to finish what they are saying and takes over the topic.

Overlapping
Two speakers talk at the same time, usually out of support and agreement with one another.

Turn-taking
The people in the conversation take it in conventional and polite turns to speak.

Context
The circumstances in which the communication takes place. This impacts greatly on the speech exchange. Speakers change their language according to the listeners and the situation.

Emphasis or stress
Words can be emphasized by being said louder or slower.

Filler
These are used in speech to fill a pause, usually to provide thinking time. For example: er, erm, like.

Jargon
Technical and specialized vocabulary related to the topic being discussed.

Pauses
Breaks in speech, sometimes filled (with fillers). Can be used for a range of reasons, such as thinking time, hesitation, indicating they want the other person(s) to contribute.

■ Infographic showing the different elements that make up spoken language

WATCH–THINK–SHARE

Refer to the infographic on page 12. Watch this short clip from the *Rob Brydon Show*, shown on the BBC, with actor, comedian and presenter, Stephen Fry: https://youtu.be/X6mPK4_3yAQ.

1 As you listen …
- **Identify** where fillers have been used. **Consider** why they have been used.
- Think about jargon. Jargon is linked to formality and technical vocabulary.
- **Identify** which words have been emphasized and why.
- **Identify** turn-taking and overlapping. How much is there and when does it occur? What causes each speaker to use one or the other?
- **Identify** each speaker's accent and dialect.
2 In pairs, **discuss** and **evaluate** the following:
- Who is the speech directed at and why?
- How formal/informal is the situation?
- How might this have affected their word choices?
- What evidence do we use from the video clip to form our impressions of the two speakers?

Find out where English is spoken around the world and where it is still the official language. Present your findings to your class by using an interactive world map template.

Here is an example for you to consider: http://youpresent.co.uk/map-templates-powerpoint/world-map-template-powerpoint/.

EXTENSION

How many different accents are there in your class?

Earlier on in the chapter we referred to different ways of speaking. Watch this short Armstrong and Miller Second World War RAF sketch: https://youtu.be/mGp4DvFEgh8.

1 As you listen …

- **Interpret** the purpose of the clip.
- **Select** the parts that you consider to be the most amusing.
- **Analyse** how language is being used.
- **Compare and contrast** the language delivery at the beginning of the clip with that in the rest of the sketch.
- **Compare and contrast** the Second World War RAF sketch with some of the programmes you listed at the start of this chapter.

2 Choose four or five different dialects from around the world and carry out some research. You can use a website like: www.dialectsarchive.com/ or any other of your choosing. Ensure you keep a record of the sources you consult.

3 Design a poster that gives information about your chosen dialects. Present your findings to your classmates.

So far in this chapter we have explored why television has captivated us since its invention and the impact it has had on shaping our perceptions of the world and to some extent, how it has influenced our use of language. In addition to this we have considered the differences between spoken and written language and carried out some simple analysis of language found in transcripts.

What is a documentary?

HOW DID DOCUMENTARY FILMMAKING GET STARTED?

■ *Man of Aran* (1934), a fictional documentary, directed by Robert J. Flaherty

■ American explorer, motion-picture director and writer, Robert J. Flaherty (1884–1951)

■ *Nanook of the North* (1922), Robert J. Flaherty's documentary of life among Inuits in Arctic Canada

ACTIVITY: Identifying a documentary

■ ATL

■ Communication skills: Organize and depict information logically

1 Refer back to the TV programme task on (page 4). In pairs, look at the TV programme list you compiled and decide which programmes are examples of documentaries. **Create** a mind map.

Hint

You could use one of these tools:
- http://popplet.com/
- https://bubbl.us/

Are documentaries a wake-up call to reality? Are they boring, or simply educational? Documentaries present facts about a subject using real events, people or places. They interpret and comment on those realities and people's concerns about them.

Thanks to the success of Michael Moore's *Fahrenheit 9/11* (2004), Davis Guggenheim's *An Inconvenient Truth* (2006) about former United States Vice President Al Gore's campaign about global warming, David Attenborough's *Life* series (which started in 1979), and most recently Professor Brian Cox's *Wonders of the Universe* (2011), the documentary has become a popular force in cinema, as well as on television.

The documentary belongs to the **expository genre**. It is a complex style containing aspects of many others. It has some features of the report genre, with its links to news reporting. It also shares some of the characteristics of the **narrative** genre; not only its intensified sense of drama and conflict, but also involvement with characters, events and settings.

2 Under each of these mind map headings, **list** your ideas in bullet points:
- **What** is a documentary?
- **When** are documentaries made?
- **What** can documentaries be about?
- **Who?** Do you know the names of any documentary stars?
- **How** are documentaries created? How are they narrated?
- **Why** are documentaries made?
- **Where?** What kinds of places do documentaries explore?

3 **Justify** your choices for why/why not the programme is/is not a documentary.
4 **Analyse** what the programmes have in common by creating a definition of what makes a documentary.
5 Thinking about a documentary you have watched and enjoyed, **identify** what it is you like about it and why.

◆ Assessment opportunities

◆ In this activity you have practised skills that are assessed using Criterion: B: Organizing and Criterion D: Using language.

The purposes of different text types

When we set out to write, it is important that we make the right choices about the **genre** and **purpose** of our texts. We need to **identify** clearly what we want to achieve, in other words, what **message** we hope to convey, and then decide which text type or genre is the most suitable for transmitting this message to its **audience.**

Look at the information on the right to help you understand which texts types are best suited for which purpose.

What are you really good at doing? Do you have any skills which others envy? Perhaps you know how to make the perfect peanut butter and jam sandwich or you know how to make a paper aeroplane. This is your opportunity to share your expertise with others.

Create a mind map of some of the things you do well and select one thing.

Write a set of instructions **explaining** how to do it.

Expository text	Information is collected and **synthesized**. The text is objective; reports are the most common type of expository text. For example, giving directions, sequencing steps, comparing one thing to another, explaining causes and effects, or describing problems and solutions belong to the expository genre.	• Autobiographies • Directions • Essays • Instructions • Posters • Recipes • Reports • Summaries
Narrative text	The text retells familiar stories and/or creates original stories. Narrative texts have a beginning, middle and end to develop the plot and characters.	• Original short stories • Personal narratives • Retellings of stories • Sequels to stories • Story scripts

ACTIVITY: Genre conventions

ATL

- Communication skills: Structure information in summaries, essays and reports
- Information literacy skills: Access information to be informed and inform others; collect, record and verify data
- Media literacy skills: Make informed choices about personal viewing experiences

Task 1

Every text has features, called **conventions**, which indicate to the reader the type of text it is. For example, if a text contained time travel, spaceships and technology, what would the genre be?

Genre is a literary category for a text. Writers create texts with varying styles, literary techniques and even lengths. Just like literature, films and TV programmes also have conventions.

In pairs, choose a programme that you like to watch and **discuss** the conventions it has.

Task 2

Documentary is a specific type of media genre, with its own specific conventions. Documentary filmmakers have developed a range of modes of shaping and presenting their material.

In groups of three, research some of the more common forms found in documentary films.

Explore the key features of two different types of documentary as listed in the table on the right. Present your research to the class. Copy the table and, as you listen to the presentations of your peers, complete the table with your notes.

Documentary modes	Key features	Examples
Expository		
Observational		
Interactive/reflexive		
Poetic/avant-garde		
Performative		
Participating		

Task 3

The channels below all show different types of documentary. Pick three documentaries from each channel and watch the first few minutes from each of the films.

Documentary channels:

- **National Geographic: https://tinyurl.com/2p8z2n7z**
- **BBC: https://tinyurl.com/a894jyyh**
- **Documentary Network: https://bit.ly/3thaMop**

1 Record the title of the documentary.
2 **Identify** the type of documentary by using your notes.
3 **Summarize** in two sentences what the documentary is about.
4 **Think** carefully about what you have seen and **evaluate** which type of documentary you like best. Make sure you can provide reasons and examples to **justify** your choice.

Assessment opportunities

- In this activity you have practised skills that are assessed using Criterion A: Analysing, Criterion B: Organizing, Criterion C: Producing text and Criterion D: Using language.

Carry out some research about other modes of documentary, such as **mockumentary**.

Give a two-minute presentation to your class on any new information you have found. Take notes as you listen to each other and **interpret** how documentary trends are evolving. Add this new information to your table.

ACTIVITY: Filmmakers and filmmaking

■ ATL

- Critical-thinking skills: Revise understanding based on new information and evidence

WATCH–THINK–SHARE

You are now going to listen to some filmmakers being interviewed.

- https://youtu.be/UEpF_AZTAzs
- https://youtu.be/hAsXwbjf7II
- https://youtu.be/XgpESPBGJL0

1 As you listen …
   - **Identify** things that are important to the filmmakers.
   - **Identify** what a documentary is – from their perspective.
2 In pairs, **discuss** and **evaluate** the following:
   - **Identify** which filmmakers are passionate about the issues they cover.
   - **Identify** which filmmakers express opinions as well as present facts about their topic.
   - **Explore** which filmmakers make films to try to persuade people to take a particular position on an issue or to inspire people to take a particular action.
   - **Select** which filmmakers want to tell a story about a unique person or event.
   - **Identify** which filmmakers use film as an art form to explore a particular subject, issue, person or event.

◆ Assessment opportunities

- ◆ In this activity you have practised skills that are assessed using Criterion A: Analysing.

■ The Lumière brothers and the birth of cinema

On 28 December 1895 the Lumière brothers projected ten short films in the basement of the Grand Café in Paris to a small paying audience of 35. This event was the birth of cinema and you could say it was the first film premiere. The reaction of the audience was astonishing. One of the films projected was *Train Arriving at the Station* and even though it was a silent film, the images were so powerful it was reported that people ran out of the basement. It just goes to show that audiences believe what they see.

The Lumières set out to create a record of life at the end of the nineteenth century. By 1897 they had created a catalogue of over 750 films. Until about 1907 non-fiction films outnumbered fiction films. These films were called 'actualities' and were mainly records of daily events. The films were shot in a single location from a stationary camera and were by no means sophisticated. There was no editing process and the films truly represented the first basic steps toward the development of the documentary as a distinct category of filmmaking.

■ John Grierson, considered by many to be the father of documentary making

It was, however, John Grierson, a Scottish filmmaker, who was first to use the term 'documentary' in 1926 for a number of films that featured real people and locations. Robert Flaherty's films *Nanook of the North* (1922), *Moana* (1926) and *Man of Aran* (1934), all of which depicted marginal and fast disappearing cultures, are early examples of the genre. In fact *Nanook of the North* is considered to be the first documentary ever made.

Grierson defined documentary as the 'creative treatment of actuality'. Although documentaries show different aspects of 'actuality' or 'real life', their 'creative treatment' of the subject matter has varied enormously throughout time.

Writing to explain

Writing to explain is a little bit like writing to inform. It is factual, but includes more detail. When you are explaining something, you have to give reasons for how or why something happens. It can also be a good idea to provide examples to help support your reasons.

Read the short paragraph below and complete the following:

- **Identify** the topic sentence and explain what the paragraph is likely to be about.
- **Identify** the parts of the text which **explain** the information we learn. (Where is the **how** and **why**?)

Alexander Fleming was a Scottish biologist who accidentally made a discovery which would change the world of medicine forever. He was investigating staphylococci when he made this discovery. During his investigation, Alexander Fleming took a holiday from his day-to-day work in the lab and, upon his return, he observed that fungus had killed off all the surrounding bacteria in the culture. He experimented further, and eventually named the substance penicillin.

DISCUSS

In pairs, **discuss** what you think Grierson meant by 'creative treatment of actuality'.

ACTIVITY: The early non-fiction filmmakers

ATL

■ Media literacy skills: Understand the impact of media representations and modes of presentation

You might be surprised to find out that, since Grierson used the phrase 'creative treatment of actuality' there have been many different interpretations and much disagreement on just how 'creative' such treatments of reality should be.

Watch five to ten minutes of each of the following films:

- **https://youtu.be/lkW14Lu1IBo**
- **https://youtu.be/41poXPVOhz0**
- **https://youtu.be/cXWxqWcqu_8.**

As you watch …

- **Identify** the topic in each film and take notes on your impressions of what Robert Flaherty was trying to achieve with his films.
- **Explore** how creative you think documentaries should be.
- **Compare and contrast** how this work is different from or similar to fictional filmmaking.

ACTIVITY: Compare and contrast a documentary and a news report

■ ATL

- Communication skills: Read critically and for comprehension; make inferences and draw conclusions

For the following activity watch the video clip: https://vimeo.com/101535600 and read this text: https://bit.ly/3oGYAtq.

In pairs, **compare and contrast** the documentary with the news report, by answering the following questions:

- **Identify** what each is about.
- **Why was it made?**
- **Who paid for it?**
- **Who made money from it?**
- **Identify** the primary sources of information.
- **How was it distributed? In other words, outline** how it was made available to the public.
- **Identify** the major techniques the producer(s) used to convey the main message(s).

◆ Assessment opportunities

- ◆ In this activity you have practised skills that are assessed using Criterion A: Analysing.

- **Identify** how you think he made his films.
- **Comment** on how this approach to non-fiction filmmaking influenced future filmmakers.
- **Justify** how our perspective changes of the people and places in the film.
- What did you make of the films? **Evaluate** how audiences would have reacted to these films when they were made.

◆ Assessment opportunities

- ◆ In this activity you have practised skills that are assessed using Criterion A: Analysing.

Perfecting paragraphs

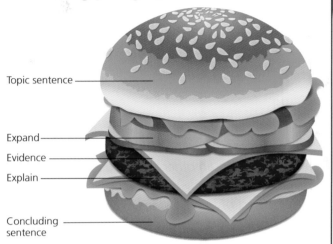

Topic sentence —
Expand —
Evidence —
Explain —
Concluding sentence —

■ Hamburger paragraph builder

When you write, it is absolutely essential that you **organize** your writing in a clear and coherent way, otherwise it can become a nightmare for your readers.

Here are some tips to help you perfect your paragraphs.

1   Decide what your paragraph is going to be about and think carefully about your **topic sentence**. A topic sentence is the first line of a paragraph and is used to introduce the main content of your paragraph. Topic sentences can help you make your writing more focused – as soon as the content of your paragraph doesn't seem to fit in with your topic sentence, then it's probably time to start a new one.

2   Make sure that you start a new paragraph when there's a change in **topic**, **time** or **location**. This gives your writing clarity and order and can help you organize your ideas more effectively.

3   Make sure that your paragraphs are made up of clear, concise sentences. Think carefully about your use of punctuation.

Let's practise writing a paragraph. Choose one of the films you watched earlier and write a paragraph about it.

How real is the reality in a documentary?

'Each medium, if its bias is properly exploited, communicates a unique aspect of reality, of truth. Each offers a different perspective, a way of seeing an otherwise hidden dimension of reality [...] A medium is not simply an envelope that carries any letter; it is itself a major part of that message.' – Edmund Carpenter, The New Languages, 1960

Why do viewers have a tendency to believe in the reality of the documentary? As spectators we are asked to trust the images and information that we are being shown. But where does this trust come from? Without a doubt, it stems from our belief as an audience in the honesty of the filmmaker, and this is where the power of the documentary comes from.

We have already looked at the conventions of documentary filmmaking, and understanding the strategies and conventions filmmakers use will help us become better critical viewers. Maintaining a critical perspective enables an audience to judge the relationship between filmed accounts and events, and those which have actually occurred in the real world.

But is seeing always believing? When we watch a documentary, we are ultimately getting a perspective – the filmmaker's perspective. We need to carefully evaluate and reflect on the information presented to us on screen in order to help form our own ideas about the topic or issue in question.

It is our role as viewers to ask questions about what we are seeing: What information has the documentary maker included and why? What is missing and is there a reason or an agenda for omitting these details?

The documentary is a powerful tool that can influence change and raise awareness. But, with power comes great responsibility, and we need to decide where this responsibility lies – with us, as viewers, or with the filmmakers themselves.

ACTIVITY: Seeing is believing

ATL

- Information literacy skills: Identify primary and secondary sources; use critical-literacy skills to analyse and interpret media communications

■ The mystery of the Loch Ness Monster

ACTIVITY: 'Crosseyed and Painless' by Talking Heads

Why do we tell stories? What's the purpose? In which different ways do we tell stories?

Songs are a great medium for telling stories. American rock band Talking Heads were formed in 1975 in New York City. Listen to their song 'Crosseyed and Painless' from their album *Remain in Light* (1980): https://youtu.be/z92avHmgDRA.

1 As you listen …
- **Identify** the tone and mood of the song in terms of its lyrics.
- **Identify** the persona or voice in the song and **comment** on what they are saying.
- What is the situation/problem/dilemma that the persona is describing?
- Do you agree with the message in the song? Why? Why not?

2 Visit this website and read from the line 'Facts are simple and facts are straight' towards the end of the song: https://bit.ly/36yIA6T.
- **Identify** the literary device the writer has used throughout. **Evaluate** the effect it has.
- **Interpret** the lyrics, and make some connections between them and what you have learnt about documentaries.
- Which is your favourite line? Explain why.

3 Now it's your turn. Write your own song lyrics and tell a story.

◆ Assessment opportunities

- In this activity you have practised skills that are assessed using Criterion A: Analysing and Criterion C: Producing text.

In the summer of 1933, a Mr Spicer and his wife were driving along on a road by Loch Ness, a large freshwater lake in the Scottish Highlands. What they claim to have encountered gave birth to a legend that has intrigued millions of people across the world for decades.

According to the Spicers, they witnessed a large, cumbersome creature, with a long elephantine neck and huge body, heading towards the water. Following their 'discovery', reports of new sightings flooded in and to this day people flock to the loch in the hope of catching a glimpse of this elusive creature, affectionately known as Nessie. Many people have claimed to have captured the Loch Ness Monster on film, but the authenticity of these pictures has been questioned.

Watch this video: https://youtu.be/o1CckgYxMS4 and answer the following questions:

1 **Analyse** how the documentary makers of the Paleoworld clip present 'truth' through tone and language. How else do they authenticate the content? Find evidence to **justify** your response.
2 **Evaluate** why the legend of Nessie has captivated the imagination of people for so long. Why are we so desperate to accept the reports?
3 How did you **evaluate** the 'truth' of the images you were presented with?
4 Are you familiar with any other legends, like that of the Loch Ness Monster, from your own country or culture?
5 Carry out some research of local legends in your country. Record and **evaluate** the sources you have used. How reliable are they? Give a two-minute presentation of your findings to your classmates.

◆ Assessment opportunities

- In this activity you have practised skills that are assessed using Criterion A: Analysing and Criterion D: Using language.

Are ethical issues central to documentary filmmaking?

When buying a DVD, the first thing we look at is the packaging. Before going to the cinema to watch a film we often watch the trailer to get a taste of the film to see whether or not it interests us. TV guides, as we have seen earlier on in the chapter, keep us up to date with what is on offer during the week.

So, what about film posters? They are vital elements of the film marketing process because they are easy to distribute. They can be placed in cinema foyers, on buses, on billboards and in magazines, giving the film maximum exposure. Promotional film posters tend to contain either a single image or a number of images that are designed to excite the audience – usually the images will show the main characters in order to draw on the popularity of certain actors or actresses to attract an audience.

ACTIVITY: The film marketing poster

■ ATL

- Communication skills: Make inferences and draw conclusions; preview and skim texts to build understanding; paraphrase accurately and concisely

When looking at still images there are two ways of decoding their content: one is to look at what they show; the second is to infer the meaning of the images.

Both of these modes of interpretation help us to understand what the film companies are trying to achieve and what effect they intend to have on the audience.

Look at the promotional film poster for *Sounds Like Teen Spirit* (see page 10 and this weblink for an alternative film poster: https://bit.ly/3apFC5D) and answer the questions:

1 **Outline** the information the promotional poster provides about the film.
2 Using only this information, **summarize** what the film is about.
3 **Identify** the information that is not included on the poster.
4 Does the information on the poster make you want to know more? Why or why not?
5 Based only on the film's title, what might you expect to learn from the film?
6 What does the film poster denote? What does it connote?

◆ Assessment opportunities

- ◆ In this activity you have practised skills that are assessed using Criterion A: Analysing and Criterion D: Using language.

ⓘ **Denotation** This is when we look at the literal meaning of an image; in other words, we comment on what is literally presented to us.

Connotation This is what is implied by the literal meaning of the images that we are looking at.

ACTIVITY: Scripting

ATL

- Creative-thinking skills: Use brainstorming and visual diagrams to generate new ideas and inquiries

Before you can script your documentary, you must first think about how your purpose, audience and **context** will affect your presentation. You must consider, for example, the images and language you will use, the way you will speak and so on. **Evaluate** what you want your audience to see and how you will make it credible. Will it change their perspectives? Use the mind map to help you.

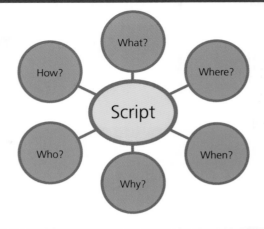

◆ Assessment opportunities

- ◆ In this activity you have practised skills that are assessed using Criterion B: Organizing and Criterion D: Using language.

ACTIVITY: Storyboards

ATL

- Creative-thinking skills: Create original works and ideas; use existing works and ideas in new ways

In groups of three, transfer your script ideas into a narrative on a storyboard. Select the visual stimulus you want to use for each piece of narration and draw a relevant image in the boxes provided.

You can use this storyboard template: **https://bit.ly/3jaf8sM** or make your own. There are other useful templates on the same website that you can use to **organize** your film.

Now have a go at writing the script for your short documentary film.

◆ Assessment opportunities

- ◆ In this activity you have practised skills that are assessed using Criterion B: Organizing and Criterion C: Producing text.

Writing a script

A script is a piece of writing in the form of drama. Drama is different from the narrative style used in novels and short stories because it is intended to be performed, on stage, radio, television or film.

Search **how to write a film script** online for guidelines on how to write a script and to view some examples.

The way that you shoot the film is an important part of getting the film right. This is also known as framing. Find out more about shot sizes, camera angles and movements: **https://bit.ly/2Mjo6YY**

Tips

- Write the speaker's name or initials on the left, in capitals, followed by a colon.
- Include directions for when and where characters should enter or exit the scene.
- Write shot directions in brackets.
- Give essential information at the start of a shot, such as a title, if necessary, where and when the scene is set and which characters are in the scene.

Make your own documentary

❗ Are there any issues you feel strongly about at your school or in your local area? Perhaps littering is a problem or maybe there aren't enough recycling bins available? Maybe you'd like to raise awareness about these problems? Or maybe you'd like to celebrate the diversity at your school?

◆ Find out where in your school you can borrow suitable equipment from to help you **create** your documentary. If you don't know how to use it, ask!

◆ Decide on a topic or issue you'd like to **explore** and then plan carefully, in specific detail. You should know exactly what you want to achieve and make a storyboard to help you **organize** your film.

◆ If you are filming or interviewing people, you *must* ask for their permission first.

◆ Perhaps you can share your documentary in an assembly.

Set up a documentary film club

❗ Don't feel ready to try your own hand at documentary making but still want to make a difference? No need to worry. Watching documentaries can be equally rewarding, so why not set up a documentary film club at lunchtime or after school?

◆ Approach a teacher who may be willing to supervise your club.

◆ Perhaps you can use *Seems Like Teen Spirit* for your first screening. If you can't watch all of it, then choose some key clips.

◆ Set time aside for reflection and **discussion** at the beginning or end of each session.

◆ Allow members of the club to nominate documentaries for future screenings. Remember, always check with a teacher to make sure that the content is suitable for your age group.

◆ Go further and take action by raising awareness about the issues that emerge in some of the documentaries you watch.

A SUMMATIVE TASK TO TRY

Use this task to apply and extend your learning in this chapter. The task is designed so that you can evaluate your learning at different levels of achievement in the Language and literature criteria.

THIS TASK CAN BE USED TO EVALUATE YOUR LEARING IN CRITERION B, CRITERION C AND CRITERION D.

Global context – Personal and cultural expression

Timing recommendation: 40 minutes

Look at this image and the one on the next page. Respond to **one** of the prompts.

■ Image 1

Imagine you are going to create a documentary about **one** of the images. Create a narrative piece of writing that will be turned into a script about what is happening, how you feel about it and why. Include why you think it would make a good documentary.

OR

Create a speech about **personal and cultural expression** for a school assembly using one of the images shown.

State the image you are using.

■ Image 2

Language and Literature for the IB MYP 1: *by Concept*

Reflection

In this chapter, we have stopped to consider the viewing choices we make as an **audience** and how our choices shape our **point of view** on what we think is true or important. We have seen how documentaries have evolved and will continue to do so. Documentaries offer an opportunity to make sense of the world through the ideas of documentarians. The most innovative examples are those made by independent directors, reporters and producers.

Use this table to reflect on your own learning in this chapter.					
Questions we asked	Answers we found	Any further questions now?			
Factual: What is a documentary? What are the conventions of a documentary? How did documentary filmmaking get started? What types of documentary are there? What different TV genres are there?					
Conceptual: How real is the reality in a documentary? How do documentary films differ from other types of films? Is language changing in film and television? What conventions are used to communicate with an audience in the genre of documentary?					
Debatable: Are ethical issues central to documentary filmmaking?					
Approaches to learning you used in this chapter:	Description – what new skills did you learn?	How well did you master the skills?			
		Novice	Learner	Practitioner	Expert
Collaboration skills					
Communication skills					
Creative-thinking skills					
Critical-thinking skills					
Information literacy skills					
Media literacy skills					
Reflection skills					
Learner profile attribute(s)	Reflect on the importance of being open-minded for your learning in this chapter.				
Open-minded					

2 Myths and legends: A mirror of reality?

For centuries we have used the **genre** of myths and legends for the **purpose** of gaining a **perspective** on human behaviour and **individual and cultural identities**.

CONSIDER THESE QUESTIONS:

Factual: What are myths and legends? What is the difference between a myth and a legend? What are the conventions of myths and legends?

Conceptual: What purpose do myths and legends fulfil? What can myths and legends reveal about human behaviour? How can we use myths and legends to make sense of our surroundings? Can sharing myths and legends help preserve our individual and cultural identities?

Debatable: Are legends based on reality? Can we create new myths? Do the same myths exist in all cultures? Is there a place for myths in the modern world? Are there modern myths?

Now **share and compare** your thoughts and ideas with your partner, or with the whole class.

IN THIS CHAPTER, WE WILL ...

■ **Find out** what myths and legends are and why they are important.

■ **Explore** how myths and legends have influenced our culture and how stories can help us to better understand the world in which we live.

■ **Take action** to preserve the tradition of storytelling.

These Approaches to Learning (ATL) skills will be useful …

- Collaboration skills
- Communication skills
- Creative-thinking skills
- Information literacy skills
- Media literacy skills
- Reflection skills

We will reflect on this learner profile attribute …

- Knowledgeable – we explore ideas of importance and dig deep into their meaning, creating a balance of our learning.

Assessment opportunities in this chapter:

- **Criterion A:** Analysing
- **Criterion B:** Organizing
- **Criterion C:** Producing text
- **Criterion D:** Using language

THINK–PUZZLE–EXPLORE

1 Consider the questions below and write your own personal responses on a sticky note:
   - What do you **think** you know about myths, legends and heroes?
   - What questions or **puzzles** do you have?
   - How can you **explore** this topic?
2 Now, in groups of three, share your ideas and questions. Negotiate which 'puzzle' questions you want to keep and write them on new sticky notes.
3 Place your 'puzzles' on a board in your classroom.
4 Brainstorm ideas on how to explore this topic.
5 Now look at the heroes, myths and legends vocabulary and definitions on this webpage: https://bit.ly/3apGiId.
6 In pairs, use an online thesaurus and find other synonyms to add to the words on the list.
7 Use a tool like https://monkeylearn.com/word-cloud/ or another word cloud generator to **create** your own extended word cloud on the topic.

KEY WORDS

classical	immortality	parable
embody	legendary	plausible
fictitious	moral	ritual
folklore	mortal	stereotypes
illusion	mythical	symbolism

What are myths and legends?

WHY DO STORIES MATTER?

Myths and legends are inextricably woven into the fabric of our culture. They help us not only to better understand the worlds we live in, but also allow us an insight into human nature. But what makes myths and legends different from other types of storytelling and why have they stood the test of time?

Perhaps it is the universality of myths and legends which makes them so appealing. As we look at myths and legends from around the world, we begin to see connections across cultures, and learn that despite our many differences, we ultimately value the same human characteristics, make the same critical errors and share the same fears and anxieties.

Some people say that all stories are built on the foundation of myth. They say that we encounter the same characters, who overcome the same obstacles, only in different **contexts**: a different time perhaps, or a different place. Maybe it is this, our ability to recognize the familiar in these old tales that makes them so attractive.

ACTIVITY: Why do myths and legends matter?

ATL

- Communication skills: Make inferences and draw conclusions

1. In pairs, **discuss** the quotes about myths and legends. Think about the following:
   - **Interpret** what each quote means.
   - **Analyse** the thoughts, feelings, ideas or attitudes about myths and legends that are being expressed in these quotes.
   - Which one do you like the most? Explain why.
2. Now, in the same pairs:
   - **Evaluate** why people think myths and legends are important.
   - Should we still read and share myths and legends? Justify your answers.
   - **Outline** what myths and legends mean to you.

◆ Assessment opportunities

- ◆ In this activity you have practised skills that are assessed using Criterion A: Analysing.

'Does progress mean that we dissolve our ancient myths? If we forget our legends, I fear that we shall close an important door to the imagination.' – *James Christensen*

'Everything we consider today to be myth and legend, our ancestors believed to be history and everything in our history includes myths and legends.' – *C. JoyBell C.*

'When we lose our myths we lose our place in the universe.' – *Madeleine L'Engle*

'A myth is a way of making sense in a senseless world. Myths are narrative patterns that give significance to our existence.' – *Rollo May*

'After all, I believe that legends and myths are largely made of "truth", and indeed present aspects of it that can only be received in this mode; and long ago certain truths and modes of this kind were discovered and must always reappear.' – *J.R.R. Tolkien*

'We need myths that will help us to identify with all our fellow-beings, not simply with those who belong to our ethnic, national or ideological tribe. We need myths that help us to realize the importance of compassion.' – *Karen Armstrong*

What is the difference between a myth and a legend?

WHAT ARE THE CONVENTIONS OF MYTHS AND LEGENDS?

How do we distinguish between a myth and legend? There is a fine line between the two and the terms are often used interchangeably. While both grew out of an oral tradition of storytelling (the word 'myth' comes from the Greek *mythos* which means 'word of mouth'), there are some key differences which can help us decide whether to categorize stories as myths or legends. Let's start with legends …

Legends are about people and their deeds, and are often rooted in history. A legend follows the life and adventures of a particular character, one who possesses heroic qualities; some details may be based on fact. However, legends cannot be relied on as real factual records of historical events as there is sometimes a strong element of fantasy in these stories, in which magic and miracles are common. Legends are tied to where they originate from and reflect the spiritual beliefs and cultural practices of these places.

Myths, on the other hand, have a purpose to fulfil or a message to convey. They can teach us how to understand our world better and can help us make more informed decisions about the way we act in certain situations, because they allow us to see the consequences of our behaviour. Myths, often more so than legends, are concerned with the realm of the imaginary and supernatural.

In this section, we'll take a closer look at the conventions of myths.

ACTIVITY: What makes a myth?

■ ATL

- Information literacy skills: Access information to be informed and inform others

1 **On the right is a list of the conventions of a myth. Copy and complete the table, matching the convention to the correct definition and completing the last column by carrying out some research.**
2 **Watch the following video and identify as many of the conventions as you can: https://youtu.be/L2tMUbB2wXY.**
3 **In pairs or groups of three, discuss the following:**
   - **What you think the message of the story is?**
   - **What is the king's fatal flaw?**
   - **Do you have a 'fatal' flaw? If so, what is it?**

◆ Assessment opportunities

- ◆ In this activity you have practised skills that are assessed using Criterion A: Analysing and Criterion B: Organizing.

Convention	Definition	Example
Gods	A lesson that is to be learnt from the story. Usually centred on human behaviour.	
Monsters	Usually the leading character in a story, who possesses noble and admirable qualities.	
Moral message	Superhuman beings who are worshipped by humans. They have power over nature and the fates of humans.	
Hero	A mental or physical weakness. Often the cause of the downfall of the leading character in a story.	
Fatal flaw	Events that are destined to take place in the future; usually beyond the control of humans.	
Fate or destiny	Imaginary creatures, which often possess ugly or frightening characteristics.	

MYTHICAL MONSTERS

One of the most appealing features of myths are the monsters which appear in them. Monsters have always had a strange power over the human imagination – they play on our deepest fears and reflect our greatest anxieties. And yet monsters are nothing more than a product of our imagination. So, why did we invent monsters? Let's take a look.

ⓘ *Monstrare*

Did you know that the word 'monster' comes from the Latin words *monstrare,* which means 'to show', and *monere,* which means 'to warn'.

What do you think stories about monsters are trying to show us or warn us about?

Read the following extract from an essay by Professor Paul Trout entitled 'Why We Invented Monsters':

Monsters fill the mythic landscape. In Hawaiian myth, there is a human with a 'shark-mouth' in the middle of his back. In Aboriginal myth, there is a creature with the body of a human, the head of a snake, and the suckers of an octopus. In South American myth, there is the were-jaguar; in Native American myth, there are flying heads, human-devouring eagles, predatory owl-men, water-cannibals, horned snakes, giant turtles, monster bats, and even a human-eating leech as large as a house. In Greek myth, one finds Polyphemus, the one-eyed cannibal giant; the Minotaur, a monstrous human-bull hybrid that consumes sacrificial victims in the 'bowels' of the subterranean Labyrinth; and Scylla, the six-headed serpent who wears a belt of dogs' heads ravenously braying for meat.

Regardless of their different sizes, features, and forms, monsters have one trait in common – they eat humans.

DISCUSS

In pairs or groups of three, **discuss** the following:

1 Were you frightened of any particular monsters when you were younger? Are there any monsters that still scare you?
2 What is your first memory of a 'monster'? Or where have you come across monsters?
3 Why are we so intrigued by monsters as human beings?

ACTIVITY: Mythical monsters

■ ATL

■ Communication skills: Read critically and for comprehension

Answer these questions after reading the extract in the previous column.

1 Identify what the writer says all monsters have in common.
2 Interpret what the opening sentence suggests about the writer's belief in the existence of monsters.
3 Analyse the descriptions of the monsters in the extract. Identify examples of language used to depict the monsters as predatory (to show that they kill and eat their prey).
4 Discuss why they writer has used examples from different places and cultures. What does this reveal about us as people?
5 Select the monster described in the text which strikes you as the most frightening. Use the description to help you create a picture of your chosen monster. Show a partner and see if they can guess which monster it is.

◆ Assessment opportunities

◆ In this activity you have practised skills that are assessed using Criterion A: Analysing and Criterion D: Using language.

Stories about a strange and terrifying sea-dwelling creature have circulated since ancient times. In Norway, this leviathan, or sea monster, is known as the **Kraken**. Sailors described the havoc wreaked on their boats by this many limbed beast of gigantic proportions which tore ships apart and devoured men whole. Today, we interpret these vivid encounters with the Kraken as exaggerated stories about giant squid, animals which still inhabit our oceans today.

■ A ship being attacked by the Kraken

ACTIVITY: The Kraken – legendary leviathans

■ ATL

- ■ Communication skills: Take effective notes in class; write for different purposes
- ■ Reflection skills: Develop new skills, techniques and strategies for effective learning

Imagine you are a member of the crew on a ship. The ship has been attacked by a Kraken.

Write a diary entry about your terrifying experience. Make sure you include plenty of description of the monster and use stylistic devices to make your writing richer.

◆ Assessment opportunities

- ◆ In this activity you have practised skills that are assessed using Criterion B: Organizing, Criterion C: Producing text and Criterion D: Using language.

Annotating texts

To get the most out of a text, you should read it actively, which means with a pencil in your hand. **Annotations** are notes or comments that you make about a text while reading it. These are particularly useful if you're reading a longer text, as your notes can help you remember the most important bits. Annotations or notes can be placed around the text, in the margins or in between the lines if there is space. You can also underline or highlight the most significant parts of the text.

When you are annotating, it's a good idea to have a focus – a clear idea of what it is that you are looking for.

Look at the **sonnet** below and see how it has been annotated with the following questions in mind. You'll notice that, to make it easier, a different colour has been used for each question.

- What stylistic devices and language features has the poet used in the poem?
- How is the Kraken described?

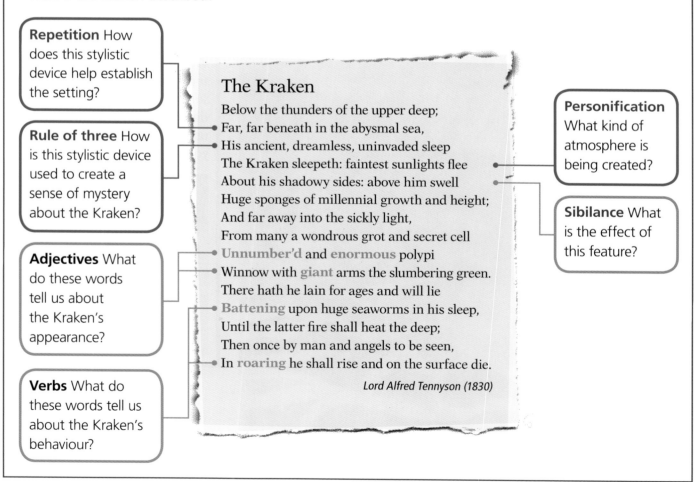

Repetition How does this stylistic device help establish the setting?

Rule of three How is this stylistic device used to create a sense of mystery about the Kraken?

Adjectives What do these words tell us about the Kraken's appearance?

Verbs What do these words tell us about the Kraken's behaviour?

Personification What kind of atmosphere is being created?

Sibilance What is the effect of this feature?

The Kraken

Below the thunders of the upper deep;
Far, far beneath in the abysmal sea,
His ancient, dreamless, uninvaded sleep
The Kraken sleepeth: faintest sunlights flee
About his shadowy sides: above him swell
Huge sponges of millennial growth and height;
And far away into the sickly light,
From many a wondrous grot and secret cell
Unnumber'd and enormous polypi
Winnow with giant arms the slumbering green.
There hath he lain for ages and will lie
Battening upon huge seaworms in his sleep,
Until the latter fire shall heat the deep;
Then once by man and angels to be seen,
In roaring he shall rise and on the surface die.

Lord Alfred Tennyson (1830)

What purpose do myths and legends fulfil?

WHAT CAN WE LEARN FROM MYTHS?

In a world where scientific thought is everywhere, there is very little that we come across on a day-to-day basis that cannot be explained by an expert somewhere. Today, we have a theory about how the world came to be, know why the sky is blue and understand how earthquakes happen – all thanks to science.

But it wasn't always like this, in times past people had to make sense of their surroundings without the help of science and technology, and had to seek out comforting explanations for the things that baffled them. Myths have filled in the gaps that might otherwise have slowed our progress as a species and have played a crucial role in our personal, social and cultural development. Interestingly enough, some of these early stories, despite being full of magic and sorcery, might have more to them than we initially thought.

Myths not only help us explain natural phenomena, but they also give as an invaluable insight into human behaviour and action; from myths we can learn important moral lessons, and understand the sometimes devastating consequences of rash action taken without enough thought. From myths we can identify the characteristics that can often lead people to their downfall; it is myths that teach us to value virtue over vice, and encourage us to live our lives as better people.

ACTIVITY: Don't fly too high!

■ ATL

- Communication skills: Read critically and for comprehension

Read the two stories of Icarus and Jatayu and Sampati (on pages 36 and 37) and then complete the following tasks:

1 **Compare and contrast** the two stories.
2 **Interpret** the stories and **identify** the main message of both.
3 **Evaluate** the effect the key difference between the two myths has on their message.
4 These stories are from two different cultures, separated by over three thousand miles. Reconsider the similarities between them and **comment** on the significance of this. What does this show about human behaviour and experience?
5 Which IB learner profile characteristics do the characters in the stories possess? Which do you think they lack? Support your answers with evidence from the texts.

◆ Assessment opportunities

- In this activity you have practised skills that are assessed using Criterion A: Analysing.

Jatayu and Sampati

Jatayu and Sampati are demi-gods in the shape of eagles who appear in the Hindu epic the *Ramayana* which is thought to date from as far back as the fifth century. They feature in the story of Rama and Sita. Here Sampati tells his story:

■ *Landscape with the Fall of Icarus* by Pieter Bruegel

We were both sons of Aruna, the charioteer of the sun god. We were very happy, skimming and floating in the higher skies. One day we decided to fly higher than ever so that we might have a glimpse of the heavens where the gods reside.

We flew together higher and higher and crossed the path of the sun god, who felt irritated at the sight of us, and when he turned his full energy in our direction, Jatayu, who was protected in the shadow of my wings, was unhurt; but my feathers and wings were all burnt and charred and I fell as a heap of bones and flesh on this mountain.

It has all along been a life of great suffering for me and I have survived because of the help of a sage who lives in this mountain.

From The Ramayana, *R.K. Narayan*

■ Jatayu and Sampati

Consider the following questions:

1 When you look at the painting (on page 36), what is your eye drawn to?

2 How do the people in the painting react to Icarus's fall? What does this say about human behaviour?

3 What point do you think Williams is making in his poem? Which words do you think express this point?

4 Does the message in Williams' poem link to the message of the Icarus myth?

Icarus and Daedalus

The story of Icarus and Daedalus is from Greek mythology. Icarus is the son of the master craftsman Daedalus, the creator of the Labyrinth. Icarus and his father attempt to escape from Crete by means of wings that his father constructed from feathers and wax. Read the full story:

https://bit.ly/3oH2tP2

The myth of Icarus is among the most popular and well known stories of Greek mythology. It has captured the interest and imagination of writers and artists across the world, and has been used time and time again in literature and visual art.

But what is the secret of its appeal? Is it the relationship between parent and child which we can relate to? Or is it the fact that it reveals a truth about our own behaviour?

Look at the painting on page 36 by Dutch painter, Pieter Bruegel. The American poet William Carlos Williams wrote an **ekphrastic poem**, inspired by the painting. An ekphrastic poem describes a scene in a painting. There is often a narrative or reflective element to it and these types of poems can help add further meaning to the artwork. Read William Carlos Williams' poem. Bruegel's interpretation of the Icarus myth dates from the mid-sixteenth century while the poem was written in the twentieth century.

Landscape With The Fall of Icarus

According to Bruegel
when Icarus fell
it was spring

a farmer was ploughing
his field
the whole pageantry

of the year was
awake tingling
near

the edge of the sea
concerned
with itself

sweating in the sun
that melted
the wings' wax

unsignificantly
off the coast
there was

a splash quite unnoticed
this was
Icarus drowning

By William Carlos Williams

EXTENSION

Search for other paintings or sculptures that are based on popular myths. If you're feeling really ambitious, you could have a go at writing your own ekphrastic poem about one that you really like.

EXTENSION ACTIVITY: Mythological biographical poem

■ ATL

- Creative-thinking skills: Create original works and ideas; use existing works and ideas in new ways

A biographical poem (or bio-poem) uses a set structure to describe the most important facts about someone.

Watch this video and select one of the Greek gods that feature in it: **https://youtu.be/eJCm8W5RZes**.

Carry out some more research to learn a little more about them.

Using the structure below, write a bio-poem about your chosen character.

Greek name …

I am (list four characteristics) …

I am a relative of …

Lover of …

Who feels/protects/believes …

Who needs …

Who fears …

Who gives …

Resident of …

Roman name …

◆ Assessment opportunities

- In this activity you have practised skills that are assessed using Criteria C: Producing text and Criteria D: Using language.

EXTENSION: SEPARATING MYTH FROM REALITY

I used to think … But now, I think …

So, how seriously should we take myths? Is there any real substance to these stories, which are so often centred on magic and mysticism? Can we use these stories to learn anything valuable about the past? The answer is yes, according to Matt Kaplan, who believes that mythology is a fictional expression of real experiences.

Watch the video: **https://youtu.be/CVo225pUaSA**.

In pairs or groups of three, take some time to reflect on what you have learnt. When we began this study of myths, you had some initial ideas about it and what it was all about. Let's take a moment to reflect on these ideas. What surprised you the most?

Take a minute to think back and then, using just a few sentences, **write down** what you used to think about myths. Begin your sentences with, '*I used to think …*'.

Now, think about how your ideas about myths have changed as a result of what we've been discussing in this chapter so far.

Again in just a few sentences **write down** what you now think about myths. Start your sentences with, '*But now, I think …*'.

So far in this chapter we have looked at the **conventions** of myths and legends and have drawn some comparisons between the two types of storytelling. We have explored the purpose that myths have fulfilled in the past and have begun to consider their relevance in the modern world and the impact they have on culture, the arts, language and literature.

Can sharing myths and legends help preserve our individual and cultural identities?

DO THE SAME MYTHS EXIST IN ALL CULTURES?

Myths fulfil a far greater function than simply helping us to understand ourselves and our surroundings. Before we began to write, these stories were passed down from one generation to the next orally and were an important means of preserving history, culture, tradition and identity. These stories have stood the test of time and still exist today, allowing us a glimpse into the lives and beliefs of our ancestors.

But it is not just the stories that have survived. Rituals and ceremonies also come from myth, and many are still practised in the modern world. Are there any rituals or ceremonies practised in your country that come from mythology? See if you can find out.

One of the most valuable aspects of sharing these stories with people from other cultures is that they allow us to make **connections**. Not only do myths and legends provide us with an opportunity to celebrate our cultural diversity, but more importantly, they highlight just how similar we are to one another despite our differences.

■ An effigy of the Hindu god Ganesha during celebrations of the festival of Chaturthi

■ Sleipnir, the eight-legged horse from Norse myth

■ Leifur Eiriksson, a legend in Reykjavik, Iceland

ACTIVITY: How the world came to be: creation myths from around the world

■ ATL

■ Creative-thinking skills: Practise flexible thinking – develop multiple opposing, contradictory and complementary arguments

CIRCLE OF VIEWPOINTS

1 In pairs or groups of three, make a mind map of the various perspectives on how the world was created.

   To begin, use the prompts below:
   - What viewpoints have people from different times held about this topic?
   - How do these viewpoints vary from place to place?
   - Who (and what) is affected by these viewpoints?
   - Who is involved?
   - Who might care?
   - What are your beliefs about the creation of the world?
   - Where do these beliefs come from? Science? Religion? Culture?

2 Now, choose one of these viewpoints and prepare to speak about the topic.

   Use the structure below to help you organize what you want to say:
   - **I am thinking of** … [the topic] … **from the point of view of** … [the viewpoint you've chosen].
   - **I think** … [describe the topic from your viewpoint. Be an actor – take on the character of your viewpoint].
   - **A question I have from this perspective is** … [ask a question from this viewpoint].

3 Our origins and the existence of the world is a topic that has fascinated people across the globe for centuries. It seems that some version of how the world came to be exists in every culture. Let's take a look at some of these creation myths.

   Follow the link below. Click on a region on the world map and watch the creation stories: https://bit.ly/3alueYw.
   - Which is your favourite creation story from the website? **Explain** why.
   - Do you notice any similarities between any of the stories? What are the key differences?
   - Is there a moral message in any of the stories? If so, what do you think these stories are trying to teach us?
   - What new ideas do you have about this topic that you did not have before?
   - What new questions do you have?

EXTENSION

What about creation stories from other countries and from other cultures? Do some research and add more stories to your own mythology world map.

◆ Assessment opportunities

- ◆ In this activity you have practised skills that are assessed using Criterion D: Using language.

Effective group work

We've all worked on group projects before and know that they do not always go to plan. As part of a group, you need to:

- listen to other points of view
- observe
- be engaged
- take notes
- ask questions.

So, what can you do to develop collaborative skills that will improve your project work? Giving roles to the different members of the group will ensure that each person is an important part of the group.

Everyone will then feel responsible for working together, and will share a common goal.

As a group, start by discussing and deciding on the different roles each one of you will have. Think about what you would like the project to achieve and evaluate the strengths of each member of the group. If you are not sure, ask your teacher to guide you through the decision-making process.

Remember that you may not always need to have someone taking on all of the roles. This will depend on the project. Also, you may want to combine some roles. It is important, however, to make these decisions before you start the project.

Group roles	Responsibility
Task leader	• Planning the task and sharing out responsibilities • Making sure everyone is included and can contribute • Making notes of the key points of the discussion and any decisions reached
Timekeeper	• Making sure everyone is aware of deadlines and checking that each group member is working on their tasks
Chairperson	• Leading discussions and debates, making sure everyone is given an opportunity to express their point of view fairly
Student – in favour of	• Putting forward an idea or viewpoint in favour of the topic
Student – against	• Putting forward an idea or viewpoint against the topic
Devil's advocate	• Questioning both positions and being deliberately controversial to generate more ideas and arguments
Presenter	• Taking the lead in presenting the group's work to others
Researcher	• Gathering information, identifying primary and secondary sources, sharing with the group (Find out what primary and secondary sources are by using Google or another search engine.)
Statistician	• Processing numerical and statistical data
IT technician	• Taking the lead in using a variety of media and formats to present the project

Decide on the roles that fit your project and add any that you think may be missing.

STOCK CHARACTERS

Time and time again, across the world, the same types of characters seem to appear in myths and legends. We call these recurring characters **stock characters** and they traditionally represent stereotypes that we are familiar with and tend to be specific to a particular type of literature. For example, in a fairytale, stock characters might include a damsel in distress, a valiant hero and a wicked witch.

Let's take, for example, the **trickster** – a stock character who appears frequently in myths. The trickster is usually quite clever, but doesn't always use their intelligence for good. Instead, they use their knowledge and wit to play tricks on others and generally cause havoc in the worlds in which they live. Popular examples include Anansi, the spider man who features in stories from all over Africa, and Loki, the Norse god of fire.

Does this repeated use of stock characters mean that, as people, we share the same admiration for certain positive characteristics, and disapproval for other less desirable traits? Are we all the same at heart, even though we might not live in the same place or speak the same language?

■ Loki, the Norse god of fire from Scandinavian mythology – the trickster is a recurring character in stories across the globe

ACTIVITY: Stock characters

■ . ATL

■ Communication skills: Use intercultural understanding to interpret communication; write for different purposes; organize and depict information logically
■ Collaboration skills: Exercise leadership and take on a variety of roles within groups; manage and resolve conflict, and work collaboratively in teams

In groups, choose one of the stock characters below and look at how they are represented in myths from around the world:

• the trickster
• the hero
• gods and goddesses
• monsters or other fantastic creatures.

Create a poster to inform others about your chosen stock character and be prepared to present your findings to the rest of your class.

Use your table from page 41 to remind you about working in groups.

In your poster presentation, you should do the following:

• **Provide a simple definition of your stock character.**
• **Find a number of examples from as many places around the world as possible.**
• **Identify the traits your characters have in common and explain what this reveals about human nature.**
• **Identify the differences between the characters.**
• **Identify the IB learner profile attributes that your characters possess and those they lack.**
• **Explore the wider significance of your stock character in myths. Consider what purpose these characters fulfil and think about how audiences/readers might react to your characters.**

◆ Assessment opportunities

◆ In this activity you have practised skills that are assessed using Criterion D: Using language.

ACTIVITY: Peer evaluation

The guidelines on how to agree on your roles when taking part in group work make us aware of the importance of developing collaborative skills. Receiving feedback is equally important as it helps us to reflect and identify areas for improvement and find appropriate ways of achieving our goals.

In pairs or groups of three, design a peer feedback sheet that you can use to give feedback to each other after the presentation of your group project task. **Discuss** the points that you would like to include. You could consider the following:
• what you liked about the project
• how the group supported each other
• changes you would suggest.

Are legends based on reality?

Despite the many similarities legends share with myths, there is one important difference between them. Legends, unlike myths, are told as a matter of history, and are set in real places and times. These elements which give legends a sense of realism are those which myths sometimes lack.

Legends, and the way in which they are told or recorded, tell us something about the communities from which they come and often reflect collective beliefs and cultural practices.

The word 'legend' comes from the Latin word *legenda* which means 'things to be read' and legends, more so than myths, tend to be written down. They are often made up of a series of tales or episodes focused on a particular figure, usually a hero. Examples include England's Robin Hood, who stole from the rich and gave to the poor, and Persia's Rostam, a mighty warrior known for his great adventures.

Even today, whether these characters are based on real historical figures or not causes much discussion, even though the magic and supernatural elements within these tales tend to make them less believable.

DISCUSS

Do you know of any legendary heroes from your country or culture? How are these stories shared? Orally or in writing? **Discuss** these questions in pairs or groups of three.

KING ARTHUR AND THE KNIGHTS OF THE ROUND TABLE

It's easy to see why the legend of King Arthur and the Knights of the Round Table is one which has captivated audiences worldwide for centuries. Intrigue and adventure, magic and mysticism, brave warriors and remarkable women all combine to make a compelling collection of stories. But the most fascinating thing about the Arthurian legend is that it has managed to divide historians on whether it is a fantastic tale born out of folklore or one based on reality.

Read this article to learn a little more about why historians feel this is a debate worth having: **https://bit.ly/3bL0Xbw**.

One of the most memorable episodes in the tales of King Arthur is that of the sword in the stone.

ACTIVITY: The sword in the stone

1 **Discuss** the following:
- What is your opinion of the legend of King Arthur? Do you think he was a real historical figure or simply a figment of our imagination?
- Does the video make you think differently about legends?

2 Read the extract from *The Sword in the Stone* on pages 46–49. Answer these questions. For each one find evidence from the text to support your answer.
- Arthur is referred to as 'the Wart' throughout the story. What do you think this reveals about his position in society at the time and how he is treated by others?
- What does the Wart experience when he first touches the sword?
- How is the sword described?
- How easy is it for Arthur to pull the sword from the stone?
- What heroic qualities does the Wart possess?
- This story is a legend. Identify the elements of fantasy and realism which it contains.

3 Now use the story and your answers to Question 2 to write a news report for your local paper about young Arthur pulling the sword from the stone.
- Decide whether your article will be published in a tabloid or a broadsheet paper. Think about your audience and the layout, style and language that you should use.
- Look back at the differences you highlighted between articles and documentaries in Chapter 1.
- What image would work well with your article?
- What do you think a news report needs to include in terms of content?
- Remember to include: a headline, who, what, why, where, when, how, topic sentences, paragraphs, connectives and quotations.

Read the extract from T.H. White's version of *The Sword in the Stone* (pages 46–49) where the young squire 'the Wart' is sent to find a sword for his master, a knight, Sir Kay, and unexpectedly finds himself to be the new King of England.

What are the conventions of news reports?

There are two types of newspapers: tabloid and broadsheet.

Tabloid	Broadsheet
Small newspaper	A larger format
Mix fact and emotion	More fact than emotion
Stories are mixed together	Text is structured clearly into sections
Extensive use of images and may focus less on the news	Focus on major world events and politics
Focus on famous celebrity stories, their private lives and scandal	Generally concerned with events in major cities of the world
Informal language, register and vocabulary	More formal language, register and vocabulary
Biased and emotional language	Impartial and objective language
Short sentences	Long sentences

'How does one get hold of a sword?' he continued. 'Where can I steal one? Could I waylay some knight, even if I am mounted on an ambling pad, and take his weapons by force? There must be some swordsmith or armourer in a great town like this, whose shop would be still open.'

He turned his mount and cantered off along the street. There was a quiet churchyard at the end of it, with a kind of square in front of the church door. In the middle of the square there was a heavy stone with an anvil on it, and a fine new sword was stuck through the anvil.

'Well,' said the Wart, 'I suppose it is some sort of war memorial, but it will have to do. I am sure nobody would grudge Kay a war memorial, if they knew his desperate straits.'

He tied his reins round a post of the lych-gate, strode up the gravel path, and took hold of the sword.

'Come, sword,' he said. 'I must cry your mercy and take you for a better cause.'

'This is extraordinary,' said the Wart. 'I feel strange when I have hold of this sword, and I notice everything much more clearly. Look at the beautiful **gargoyles** of the church, and of the monastery which it belongs to. See how splendidly all the famous banners in the aisle are waving. How nobly that yew holds up the red flakes of its timbers to worship God. How clean the snow is. I can smell something like fetherfew and sweet briar – and is it music that I hear?'

It was music, whether of pan-pipes or of recorders, and the light in the churchyard was so clear, without being dazzling, that one could have picked a pin out twenty yards away.

'There is something in this place,' said the Wart. 'There are people. Oh, people, what do you want?'

Nobody answered him, but the music was loud and the light beautiful.

'People,' cried the Wart, 'I must take this sword. It is not for me, but for Kay. I will bring it back.'

There was still no answer, and Wart turned back to the anvil. He saw the golden letters, which he did not read, and the jewels on the pommel, flashing in the lovely light.

'Come, sword,' said the Wart.

He took hold of the handles with both hands, and strained against the stone. There was a melodious **consort** on the recorders, but nothing moved.

The Wart let go of the handles, when they were beginning to bite into the palms of his hands, and stepped back, seeing stars.

'It is well fixed,' he said.

He took hold of it again and pulled with all his might. The music played more strongly, and the light all about the churchyard glowed like amethysts; but the sword still stuck.

'Oh, Merlyn,' cried the Wart, 'help me to get this weapon.'

There was a kind of rushing noise, and a long chord played along with it. All round the churchyard there were hundreds of old friends. They rose over the church wall all together, like the Punch and Judy ghosts of remembered days, and there were badgers and nightingales and vulgar crows and hares and wild geese and falcons and fishes and dogs and dainty unicorns and solitary wasps and **corkindrills** and hedgehogs and griffins and the thousand other animals he had met. They loomed round the church wall, the lovers and helpers of the Wart, and they all spoke solemnly in turn. Some of them had come from the banners in the church, where they were painted in heraldry, some from the waters and the sky and the fields about – but all, down to the smallest shrew mouse, had come to help on account of love. Wart felt his power grow.

'Put your back into it,' said a Luce (or pike) off one of the heraldic banners, 'as you once did when I was going to snap you up. Remember that power springs from the nape of the neck.'

'What about those forearms,' asked a Badger gravely, 'that are held together by a chest? Come along, my dear embryo, and find your tool.'

A Merlin sitting at the top of the yew tree cried out, 'Now then, Captain Wart, what is the first law of the foot? I thought I once heard something about never letting go?'

'Don't work like a stalling woodpecker,' urged a Tawny Owl affectionately. 'Keep up a steady effort, my duck, and you will have it yet.'

A white-front said, 'Now, Wart, if you were once able to fly the great North Sea, surely you can co-ordinate a few little wing-muscles here and there? Fold your powers together, with the spirit of your mind, and it will come out like butter. Come along, Homo sapiens, for all we humble friends of yours are waiting here to cheer.'

The Wart walked up to the great sword for the third time. He put out his right hand softly and drew it out as gently as from a **scabbard**.

There was a lot of cheering, a noise like a hurdy-gurdy which went on and on. In the middle of this noise, after a long time, he saw Kay and gave him the sword. The people at the tournament were making a frightful row.

'But this is not my sword,' said Sir Kay.

'It was the only one I could get,' said the Wart. 'The inn was locked.'

'It is a nice-looking sword. Where did you get it?'

'I found it stuck in a stone, outside a church.'

Sir Kay had been watching the **tilting** nervously, waiting for his turn. He had not paid much attention to his squire.

'That is a funny place to find one,' he said.

'Yes, it was stuck through an anvil.'

'What?' cried Sir Kay, suddenly rounding upon him. 'Did you just say this sword was stuck in a stone?'

'It was,' said the Wart. 'It was a sort of war memorial.'

Sir Kay stared at him for several seconds in amazement, opened his mouth, shut it again, licked his lips, then turned his back and plunged through the crowd. He was looking for Sir Ector, and the Wart followed after him.

'Father,' cried Sir Kay, 'come here a moment.'

'Yes, my boy,' said Sir Ector. 'Splendid falls these professional chaps do manage. Why, what's the matter, Kay? You look as white as a sheet.'

'Do you remember that sword which the King of England would pull out?'

'Yes.'

'Well, here it is. I have it. It is in my hand. I pulled it out.'

Sir Ector did not say anything silly. He looked at Kay and he looked at the Wart. Then he stared at Kay again, long and lovingly, and said, 'We will go back to the church.'

'Now then, Kay,' he said, when they were at the church door. He looked at his first-born kindly, but straight between the eyes. 'Here is the stone, and you have the sword. It will make you the King of England. You are my son that I am proud of, and always will be, whatever you do. Will you promise me that you took it out by your own might?'

Kay looked at his father. He also looked at the Wart and at the sword.

Then he handed the sword to the Wart quite quietly.

He said, 'I am a liar. Wart pulled it out.'

As far as the Wart was concerned, there was a time after this in which Sir Ector kept telling him to put the sword back into the stone – which he did – and in which Sir Ector and Kay then vainly tried to take it out. The Wart took it out for them, and stuck it back again once or twice. After this, there was another time which was more painful.

He saw that his dear guardian was looking quite old and powerless, and that he was kneeling down with difficulty on a **gouty** knee.

'Sir,' said Sir Ector, without looking up, although he was speaking to his own boy.

'Please do not do this, father,' said the Wart, kneeling down also. 'Let me help you up, Sir Ector, because you are making me unhappy.'

'Nay, nay, my lord,' said Sir Ector, with some very feeble old tears. 'I was never your father nor of your blood, but I wote well ye are of an higher blood than I wend ye were.'

'Plenty of people have told me you are not my father,' said the Wart, 'but it does not matter a bit.'

'Sir,' said Sir Ector humbly, 'will ye be my good and gracious lord when ye are King?'

'Don't!' said the Wart.

'Sir,' said Sir Ector, 'I will ask no more of you but that you will make my son, your foster-brother, Sir Kay, seneschal of all your lands?'

Kay was kneeling down too, and it was more than the Wart could bear.

'Oh, do stop,' he cried. 'Of course he can be **seneschal**, if I have got to be this King, and, oh, father, don't kneel down like that, because it breaks my heart. Please get up, Sir Ector, and don't make everything so horrible. Oh, dear, oh, dear, I wish I had never seen that filthy sword at all.'

And the Wart also burst into tears.

ⓘ **gargoyle** a carved statue of a creature that stands out from a building

consort an accompaniment, a supporting musical part

corkindrill a mythical creature that looks similar to a crocodile

scabbard a cover for the blade of a sword

tilting charging at something with a lance or a sword

gouty afflicted with gout, a disease that affects the foot

seneschal a person in charge of running a domestic household

Is there a place for myths in the modern world?

What is it about myths and legends which has ensured their survival in the modern age? Yes, the stories are still as captivating as they were hundreds of years ago when they first appeared, but it is also their ability to change and adapt, and today we find ourselves surrounded by 'modern myths'.

The usage of the terms 'myth' and 'legend' have changed. Today, we often use the word 'legend' to describe people, often celebrities, who have excelled in their particular field and deserve respect – Mohammed Ali, for example, is considered a boxing legend, but we don't for a moment doubt that he existed.

The word 'myth' is used to talk about things which most people believe, but are probably untrue. For example, has your mum or teacher ever told you that if you swallow chewing gum, it'll take you seven years to digest it? Well, you can rest assured that although it will take a little bit longer to break down than most other foods, it won't take seven years – it's a myth!

Modern myths and legends are springing up around us every day – take urban legends, for example, which play on modern fears and anxieties. These are stories (usually rather gruesome ones) you might have heard in your local area from older friends and family members who will swear they 'know someone it happened to'.

It seems that our fascination with myths and legends is here to stay, so let's take a look at myths in the modern world.

Rick Riordan's bestselling series of novels, *Percy Jackson and the Olympians*, are set in the present day but centre on the adventures of Percy Jackson, a young demi-god.

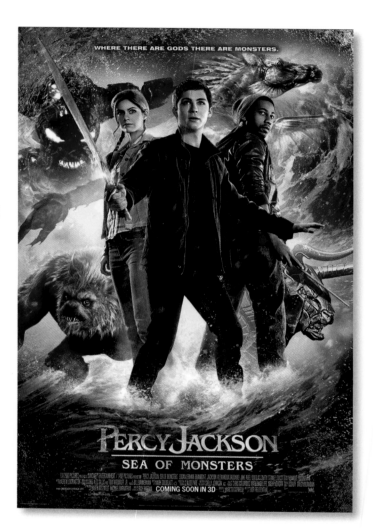

ACTIVITY: Reinventing myths

1 Watch this short video of author Rick Riordan talking about the Percy Jackson series: https://youtu.be/itcTiQEVIo0.

2 **Summarize the content in no more than** *five* **bullet points or sentences. Look at the 'Six steps to effective summarizing or synthesizing' on page 53 for tips.**

3 Then, in pairs or groups of three, **discuss** what he says about the appeal of myths.

4 Read the extract below and answer these questions:

- What revelation does Chiron make?
- Which mythical creatures are mentioned in the extract?
- What is Mr D's attitude towards mortals?
- What do we learn about Grover in the extract? What techniques does the writer use to establish his character?
- What conventions of myth can you **identify** in the extract?
- How does Percy's perspective change over the course of the extract?

Read this extract from the novel:

Chiron smiled at me sympathetically, the way he used to in Latin class, as if to let me know that no matter what my average was, I was his star student. He expected me to have the right answer.

'Percy,' he said. 'Did your mother tell you nothing?'

'She said …' I remembered her sad eyes, looking out over the sea. 'She told me she was afraid to send me here, even though my father had wanted her to. She said that once I was here, I probably couldn't leave. She wanted to keep me close to her.'

'Typical,' Mr D said. 'That's how they usually get killed. Young man, are you bidding or not?'

'What?' I asked.

He explained, impatiently, how you bid in **pinochle**, and so I did.

'I'm afraid there's too much to tell,' Chiron said. 'I'm afraid our usual orientation film won't be sufficient.'

'Orientation film?' I asked.

'No,' Chiron decided. 'Well, Percy. You know your friend Grover is a **satyr**. You know' – he pointed to the horn in the shoe box – 'that you have killed the **Minotaur**. No small feat, either, lad. What you may not know is that great powers are at work in your life. Gods – the forces you call the Greek gods – are very much alive.'

I stared at the others around the table.

I waited for somebody to yell, 'Not!' But all I got was Mr D yelling, 'Oh, a royal marriage. Trick! Trick!' He cackled as he tallied up his points.

'Mr D,' Grover asked timidly, 'if you're not going to eat it, could I have your Diet Coke can?'

'Eh? Oh, all right.'

Grover bit a huge shard out of the empty aluminum can and chewed it mournfully.

'Wait,' I told Chiron. 'You're telling me there's such a thing as God.'

'Well, now,' Chiron said. 'God – capital G, God. That's a different matter altogether. We shan't deal with the **metaphysical**.'

'Metaphysical? But you were just talking about –'

'Ah, gods, plural, as in, great beings that control the forces of nature and human endeavors: the immortal gods of Olympus. That's a smaller matter.'

'Smaller?'

'Yes, quite. The gods we discussed in Latin class.'

'Zeus,' I said. 'Hera. Apollo. You mean them.'

And there it was again – distant thunder on a cloudless day.

'Young man,' said Mr D, 'I would really be less casual about throwing those names around, if I were you.'

'But they're stories,' I said. 'They're – myths, to explain lightning and the seasons and stuff. They're what people believed before there was science.'

'Science!' Mr D scoffed. 'And tell me, Perseus Jackson' – I flinched when he said my real name, which I never told anybody – 'what will people think of your "science" two thousand years from now?' Mr D continued. 'Hmm? They will call it primitive mumbo jumbo. That's what. Oh, I love mortals – they have absolutely no sense of perspective. They think they've come so-o-o far. And have they, Chiron? Look at this boy and tell me.'

I wasn't liking Mr D much, but there was something about the way he called me mortal, as if … he wasn't. It was enough to put a lump in my throat, to suggest why Grover was dutifully minding his cards, chewing his soda can, and keeping his mouth shut.

'Percy,' Chiron said, 'you may choose to believe or not, but the fact is that immortal means immortal. Can you imagine that for a moment, never dying? Never fading? Existing, just as you are, for all time?'

I was about to answer, off the top of my head, that it sounded like a pretty good deal, but the tone of Chiron's voice made me hesitate.

'You mean, whether people believed in you or not,' I said.

'Exactly,' Chiron agreed. 'If you were a god, how would you like being called a myth, an old story to explain lightning? What if I told you, Perseus Jackson, that someday people would call you a myth, just created to explain how little boys can get over losing their mothers?'

My heart pounded. He was trying to make me angry for some reason, but I wasn't going to let him. I said, 'I wouldn't like it. But I don't believe in gods.'

'Oh, you'd better,' Mr D murmured. 'Before one of them incinerates you.'

Grover said, 'P-please, sir. He's just lost his mother. He's in shock.'

'A lucky thing, too,' Mr D grumbled, playing a card. 'Bad enough I'm confined to this miserable job, working with boys who don't even believe!'

He waved his hand and a goblet appeared on the table, as if the sunlight had bent, momentarily, and woven the air into glass. The goblet filled itself with red wine.

My jaw dropped, but Chiron hardly looked up.

ⓘ **pinochle** a card game

satyr a mythical creature, half human and half goat

Minotaur a mythical monster, part man part bull

metaphysical relating to ideas and things that are not part of the physical world

Narrative voice – First or third?

All stories are told from a particular perspective. In first person narratives, the story is told from the viewpoint of a character who speaks or writes directly, using **first person pronouns** such as 'I' or 'we'.

In a third person narrative, the story is told using third person pronouns such as 'he', 'she', 'it' or 'they'.

Third person narrative voice can be:

- **Omniscient** – An omniscient narrator is 'outside' of the story to some extent. An omniscient narrator has knowledge of all times, people, places and events, including all characters' thoughts.

- **'Over the shoulder'** – The narrator only describes the events as they occur. They don't have access to past events or what may happen in the future.

What kind of narrator is Percy Jackson?

In pairs, or groups of three, consider the advantages and disadvantages of using first and third person narratives.

Six steps to effective summarizing or synthesizing

Summarizing or **synthesizing** means presenting the main points of a topic in a shortened form. Like note taking, it is a technique that needs practice and can help you to study.

When you summarize you leave out many of the details, illustrations and examples. A good way to **summarize** is to select key words and use short sentences. It can be a lot of fun because you can put information into a new, creative form.

A good summary should be about half the length of the original text.

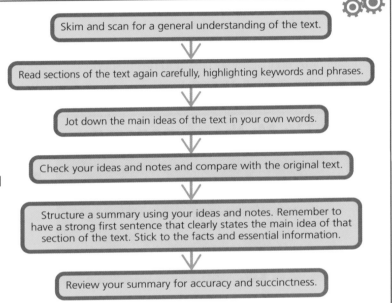

Skim and scan for a general understanding of the text.

↓

Read sections of the text again carefully, highlighting keywords and phrases.

↓

Jot down the main ideas of the text in your own words.

↓

Check your ideas and notes and compare with the original text.

↓

Structure a summary using your ideas and notes. Remember to have a strong first sentence that clearly states the main idea of that section of the text. Stick to the facts and essential information.

↓

Review your summary for accuracy and succinctness.

COMIC BOOKS AND SUPERHEROES

'They're our Greek myths, but the difference is, they're no longer what the Greek myths were to the Greeks – they're what they were to western civilisation centuries later.' – Laurence Maslon, the author of Superheroes!: Capes, Cowls, and the Creation of Comic Book Culture

'We love our superheroes because they refuse to give up on us. We can analyse them out of existence, kill them, ban them, mock them, and still they return, patiently reminding us of who we are and what we wish we could be.' – Grant Morrison, acclaimed comic book writer

Every year, the comic book industry makes a great deal of money. Although first introduced in the late nineteenth century, comic books gained popularity in the 1930s and it was then, following the birth of a hero, that they evolved into what we know them as today. Superman, the brainchild of writer Jerry Siegel and artist Joe Shuster, was an instant success and has helped shaped our ideas of what a superhero is.

In today's world, superheroes have become dominant cultural figures. They have moved from the pages of comic books onto the big screen. Characters such as Superman, Batman and Wonder Woman are household names and we can't seem to get enough of them.

But it's not all fun and games, and like myths, comics can fulfil a greater purpose. Quite often the stories reflect the concerns of the period in which they are written. For instance, in the late 1930s with the onset of the Second World War, Superman and other heroes often battled with Nazis – an issue the American public would have been worried about.

ACTIVITY: Myths of modernity

■ ATL

- Media literacy skills: Compare, contrast and draw connections among (multi)media resources
- Information literacy skills: Use critical-literacy skills to analyse and interpret media communications

1 Consider the quotes about superheroes and comic books (on page 53) and in pairs or groups of three, **discuss** the following:
  - What is a comic? How do comics differ from other types of literature? Why are they so popular?
  - Do you read any comic books? Or have you watched any movies based on comics?
  - How do you feel about the characters and stories in these books or films?
  - What is a superhero? Which qualities do superheroes need to have?
  - Why are there more male superheroes? Why is this is a problem?

2 So, are superheroes the gods and demi-gods of the modern age? Have they replaced the heroes of old? Let's see how they compare.
  Carry out some research and **compare and contrast** Achilles, a warrior from Greek mythology, with Superman. Copy and complete the table below:

	Achilles	Superman
Origins: Where are they from? What do we know about their past?		
Personality and appearance: What characteristics do they have? What do they look like?		
Fatal flaw: Do they have any weaknesses? What is the story behind this flaw?		
Secrets: Do they have any closely guarded secrets? If so, for what purpose?		
Arch-enemy: Do they have an enemy/enemies?		

3 **Identify** who you think is the better character of the two.
  Write a short paragraph explaining why. Make sure you **justify** your answer with evidence.

◆ Assessment opportunities

- ◆ In this activity you have practised skills that are assessed using Criterion A: Analysing and Criterion D: Using language.

What makes a superhero? Let's take a look:

They should be inherently good …

Well, we often find that in the comic book universe, the lines between good and evil are sometimes blurred. In fact, Superman started out life as a villain before his creators decided that he'd have more appeal as a good guy. As readers, or indeed viewers, we're not always sure how we should feel about the decisions made by comic book characters, and like the gods and heroes of mythology, they often have a 'fatal flaw'.

They have superpowers …

Yes, and no! While superheroes should, as the name suggests, possess superhuman powers, this doesn't seem to be an essential requirement and many of the superheroes in the pages of comic books are like us – mere mortals. It's not their powers, but their actions, that are extraordinary. Perhaps this is what makes them so appealing? Can you think of any superheroes who don't have superhuman powers?

They usually have a secret identity …

Imagine how difficult it would be to fit in at your school if you were a superhero. Best to keep it a secret. Many, but not all, superheroes have an alter ego that they use in order to conduct their day-to-day lives in peace. It also enables them to protect themselves and their loved ones.

They have an arch-enemy …

Superheroes tend to spend a considerable amount of time keeping a supervillain in check for the benefit of mankind. Besides, having an enemy can make a story more interesting, and that's never a bad thing!

ACTIVITY: Create your own superhero

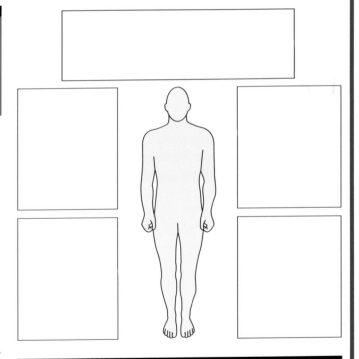

■ ATL

■ Creative-thinking skills: Use brainstorming and visual diagrams to generate new ideas and inquiries; create original works and ideas; use existing works and ideas in new ways

1 **What issues are you most worried about today? Take a few minutes to discuss this in pairs and create a mind map.**
2 **Wouldn't it be great if there was a superhero who could deal with these issues?**
   Select one issue from your mind map and copy the template to create your very own superhero. Use the boxes to annotate your superhero with the following questions in mind:
   ● **What is your superhero's name?**
   ● **Is your superhero male or female?**
   ● **What is their backstory? Where are they from?**
   ● **What superpowers do they have? How did they get these powers?**
   ● **What is their fatal flaw?**
   ● **Which IB learner profile attributes do they have?**

◆ Assessment opportunities

◆ In this activity you have practised skills that are assessed using Criterion D: Using language.

! We can all do our bit to help keep our love for myths and legends alive. Here are some fun ways in which you can make a difference ...

- ◆ **Preserve the art of storytelling:** Why not organize a myths and legends storytelling club? You could meet regularly and each week nominate a member of the club to share a story from their country or culture.

- ◆ **Raise awareness of important issues through comics:** Get together with other members of your class and use the comic book superheroes you've created to make your own comic book. You could raise awareness about littering, bullying or any other issues you feel strongly about at school.

- ◆ **Get your whole school involved:** You could create a myths and legends mural at your school to celebrate cultural diversity or organize a whole-school assembly in which stories from around the world are acted out.

A SUMMATIVE TASK TO TRY

Use this task to apply and extend your learning in this chapter. The task is designed so that you can evaluate your learning at different levels of achievement in the Language and literature criteria.

THIS TASK CAN BE USED TO EVALUATE YOUR LEARNING IN CRITERION B, CRITERION C AND CRITERION D

Modern-day myths

Timing recommendation: 60 minutes

Select one of the myths which we have explored in this chapter. Ideally, it should have a message or moral from which the reader can learn something.

Re-write the myth, but in a modern setting or context and aimed at an audience of your age. Think carefully about your choice of narrative **voice**.

Reflection

In this chapter we have explored the **conventions** of myths and legends and considered the **purpose** they fulfil in our lives; we have learnt that myths and legends give us **perspective** and help us develop a better understanding of the world in which we live, and teach us about the consequences of human action. In addition, we have considered the role that myths and legends play in preserving culture and traditions and how we can make connections with others through sharing these stories.

Use this table to reflect on your own learning in this chapter.					
Questions we asked	**Answers we found**	**Any further questions now?**			
Factual: What are myths and legends? What is the difference between a myth and a legend? What are the conventions of myths and legends?					
Conceptual: What purpose do myths and legends fulfil? What can myths and legends reveal about human behaviour? How can we use myths and legends to make sense of our surroundings? Can sharing myths and legends help preserve our individual and cultural identities?					
Debatable: Are legends based on reality? Can we create new myths? Do the same myths exist in all cultures? Is there a place for myths in the modern world? Are there modern myths?					
Approaches to learning you used in this chapter:	Description – what new skills did you learn?	How well did you master the skills?			
		Novice	Learner	Practitioner	Expert
Collaboration skills					
Communication skills					
Creative-thinking skills					
Information literacy skills					
Media literary skills					
Reflection skills					
Learner profile attribute(s)	*Reflect on the importance of being knowledgeable for your learning in this chapter.*				
Knowledgeable					

③ Do you believe in magic?

In some **genres**, writers are able to use their **creativity** to transgress the bounds of **space and time** through exploring familiar **themes** in unfamiliar **settings**.

'Fantasy is hardly an escape from reality. It's a way of understanding it.' – Lloyd Alexander

CONSIDER THESE QUESTIONS:

Factual: What is fantasy? How can you identify a fantasy story? How is fantasy different from other genres?

Conceptual: What does fantastic fiction reveal about the human imagination? Can we use fantasy to escape? How does life in the fantasy world help us learn about the real world?

Debatable: Why do we create? What does fantastic fiction reveal about the human imagination?

Now **share** and **compare** your thoughts and ideas with your partner, or with the whole class.

IN THIS CHAPTER, WE WILL …

- **Find out** what fantasy is and how escaping to other worlds can sometimes help us to cope better with issues in our day-to-day lives.
- **Explore** how authors can use language and imagery to enable us, as readers, to enter the world of fantasy.
- **Take action** to revive our love for some of the great fantasy classics in literature and to encourage ourselves and others to be open-minded about new stories of the genre that are published, some of which will go on to become classics too.

● We will reflect on this learner profile attribute …

- Thinkers – we apply thinking skills that allow us to tackle complex problems in creative ways.

KEY WORDS

character	plot
climate	setting
imagination	theme
magic	

'I like nonsense, it wakes up the brain cells. Fantasy is a necessary ingredient in living.' – Dr Seuss

'The fantastic must be so close to the real that you almost have to believe in it.' – Fyodor Dostoevsky

'Reality is not always probable, or likely.' – Jorge Luis Borges

■ These Approaches to Learning (ATL) skills will be useful …

- Collaboration skills
- Communication skills
- Creative-thinking skills
- Critical-thinking skills
- Information literacy skills
- Organization skills
- Reflection skills

◆ Assessment opportunities in this chapter:

- **Criterion A:** Analysing
- **Criterion B:** Organizing
- **Criterion C:** Producing text
- **Criterion D:** Using language

THINK–PUZZLE–EXPLORE

1 Share some of your thoughts about the questions below and write your individual responses on sticky notes. Add them to a class list of ideas.
   - What do you think you know about fantasy fiction?
   - What questions or puzzles do you have?
   - How can you explore this topic?
2 What are the motifs of the fantasy genre? A **motif** is a recurring theme, item or symbol that is typical of a particular genre.
3 Watch the following trailers. As you watch, **write down** words and phrases linked to the images that you see. Use a tool like https://monkeylearn.com/word-cloud/ or another word cloud generator to **create** a word bank on the genre of fantasy.
   - https://youtu.be/ax-Np0IdRuM
   - https://youtu.be/B1mHLQYwVX4

What is fantasy?

■ C.S. Lewis statue in Belfast, celebrating *The Lion, the Witch and the Wardrobe*

Can you remember the first fantasy book you ever read? For me, it was *The Lion, the Witch and the Wardrobe* from *The Chronicles of Narnia* by C.S. Lewis. As I read, the landscapes of Narnia, full of incredible creatures in a world that was believable, transported me to a place that I could only ever have seen in my dreams. Of course, deep down, I recognized that none of this was possible, but to me, a child limited only by my imagination, the setting and characters seemed vivid, exciting and real. Each time I picked up my book I was eager to escape into the magical world conjured up by Lewis' pen.

So, what exactly is fantasy? Well, most people find it quite difficult to define. Perhaps this is because literature is all about interpretation and we each interpret things in different ways. The literary genre of the fantastic is, however, linked to a particular type of narrative and is often confused with other genres, such as science fiction or horror. In fact, the word 'fantastic' has been used in such varied contexts that it has lost much of its original meaning.

The Weirdstone of Brisingamen: A Tale of Alderley by Alan Garner

The author Alan Garner is best known for his children's fantasy novels and his retellings of British folk tales. He started to write his first novel when he moved into a medieval house, Toad Hall in Blackden, Cheshire in the UK (shown above). The plot is influenced by the local legend of the Wizard of the Edge, and the folklore and landscape of Alderley Edge, the neighbouring area where Garner grew up.

The novel tells the story of Colin and Susan who are staying with some old friends of their mother while their parents are overseas. Susan has a bracelet with a small tear-shaped jewel – the weirdstone of the title of the book.

Despite this apparent confusion, Tzvetan Todorov made a clear distinction about fantasy in the introduction to his book, *The Fantastic: A structural approach to a literary genre*, published in 1975. Todorov identifies three categories within the fantastic genre: magical, unusual and fantastic. Each of these genres focuses on explaining the unexplainable through storytelling.

In this chapter, we will consider the magic of fantasy through a selection of texts and through the reading of a whole text, *The Weirdstone of Brisingamen: A Tale of Alderley* by Alan Garner.

First of all, get your own copy of *The Weirdstone of Brisingamen* and start reading. You can listen to the audio book if you prefer – just make sure it's an unabridged version. Use the guidelines on 'Tips on how to read a story' on page 61 to help you work with different elements of the story.

Tips on how to read a story

By checking your understanding of the text as you read, you will develop valuable strategies to help you with analysing texts. By predicting, questioning, clarifying, summarizing, connecting and evaluating as you read, you are carrying out a conversation with the author.

Pre-reading

Look at the title of the story. What might this story be about?

How can you use your background knowledge to understand the subject of the story? What questions could you ask about the title? For example, where might Brisingamen be?

What's the purpose of reading the story? Go back to the beginning of this chapter (see page 58) and select a couple of questions from the factual, conceptual and debatable list, or come up with your own. These will help you determine what is important while you read the story.

What kind of story is it? Flick through the book quickly. How many chapters does it have? Take a look at the opening sentences of different paragraphs, skim and scan through the opening paragraph. This will give you a sense of where the story is set, how difficult the language is, and how long you might need to read the story.

During reading

Identify the main characters. These are the characters that make the story happen or to whom important things happen. It is important to get to know what they are like. You could do this by asking questions, for example: *What does this character want to do and why?*

Identify the plot or situation. The plot of the story is 'what happens' in a story, in other words, the storyline. For example, in *The Lion, the Witch and the Wardrobe*, the Ice Queen wants to have complete rule over Narnia and kill Aslan. Sometimes writers prefer to put their characters in a situation. For example, in *The Maze Runner*, a group of boys are living on the outskirts of a maze and try to find a way out.

Notice the setting. Setting refers not only to where the story takes place, but when it happens. It also includes details such as tone and mood. Does the story have a scary or lonely feeling? What does the story sound like?

Evaluate the story's point of view. Why did the author choose to tell the story through a specific character's point of view? Why not a different character? How does this influence the plot? Think about the language: why has the author used the past or present tense? Look back at page 53 and review the first or third person narrative.

Pay attention to the author's use of time. How does the author use time in the story? Does the story take place in a day, a year or longer? Look for specific time words that signal time has passed.

Identify the climax. Every plot has an element of suspense, conflict or tension which comes to a head at some point. This is the moment when the character or the plot suddenly changes direction and things start to unravel differently. This is called the climax.

Remember why you are reading the story. It's important to keep sight of why you are reading the story. Refer back to the question(s) you chose when you started reading. This will help you **evaluate**.

Post-reading

First, read to understand and then, to analyse. To check that you understand what has happened, ask yourself the following questions: *who* did *what* to *whom* and *why*? Answering these questions will give you the basic details to **analyse** the story in depth.

Revisit the title. Go back to the title. How does it relate to the story now that you have read it? What does the title refer to? Does the title have more than one possible meaning? Is it a good title for the book? Why? Why not?

How is fantasy different from other genres?

Genre is the name given to a particular type of writing with its own typical features. In the introduction to this chapter, you watched several trailers and identified some of the recognizable features of the fantasy genre.

These elements vary from mythical beasts roaming an imagined world, to natural settings in which animals take on human characteristics. There are seven recognizable themes in fantasy:

- magic
- other worlds
- universal themes, for example, good vs evil
- heroism
- special character types
- articulate animals (animals that can speak)
- fantastic objects.

A story needs to have one or more of these features in order to be classified as fantasy.

A **sub-genre** is a category of the main genre, for example, super-hero fantasy is a sub-genre of heroism.

Can you see now why fantasy can be confusing? There are so many different types and the genre is still growing.

ACTIVITY: How is fantasy different from other genres?

ATL

- Communication skills: Structure information in summaries, essays and reports; give and receive meaningful feedback; organize and depict information logically
- Creative-thinking skills: Use brainstorming and visual diagrams to generate new ideas and inquiries
- Reflection skills: (Re)considering the process of learning; choosing and using ATL skills; Consider content

So what really makes 'fantasy' fantasy?

1. Watch this video https://youtu.be/n_cqszvdTqk and make notes. Go back to page 34 (Annotating texts) and review the guidelines on how to make good notes.
2. Take some time to reflect on what you have learnt. Can you relate to anything that was said in the video? What surprised you the most?
3. In pairs or groups of three, **compare and contrast** your notes. Decide which key points to keep and write a summary.
4. Now, brainstorm the titles of books and films that you have read and seen and that belong to each of the following popular fiction genres: science fiction, horror and crime. **Create** a mind map to collate your information.

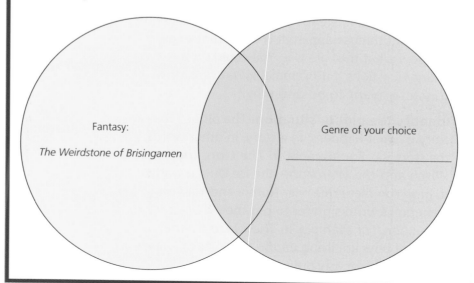

Fantasy:

The Weirdstone of Brisingamen

Genre of your choice

_____

5 Carry out some more research to learn a little more about them.

For example, motifs of crime fiction will include things that you can see, such as forensics, police, evidence linked to the crime scene, but also abstract things like revenge, fear, trauma and resolution.

6 Use a Venn diagram to **compare and contrast** the fantasy genre with another genre.

7 **Organize** all the information you have gathered on how fantasy is different from other genres and prepare a three-minute presentation to give to your classmates. **Evaluate** and select the best information sources and use a digital tool, such as Prezi or PowerPoint, to support your presentation.

ACTIVITY: How can you identify a fantasy story?

ATL

■ Communication skills: Read critically and for comprehension; use and interpret a range of discipline-specific terms and symbols

1 **Identify** what types of opening you know and what you know about writing good openings to stories. Share your thoughts with your partner.
2 Now read the opening paragraph to *The Weirdstone of Brisingamen* (see below).

In pairs, as you read, **discuss**:
● what it hints at
● how it draws the reader in
● how there are elements of the plot, character and setting in the introductory paragraph.

At dawn one still October day in the long ago of the world, across the hill of Alderley, a farmer from Mobberley was riding to the Macclesfield fair. The morning was dull, but mild; light mists bedimmed his way; the woods were hushed; the day promised fine. The farmer was in good spirits, and let his horse, a milk-white mare, set her own pace, for he wanted to arrive fresh for the market. A rich man would walk back to Mobberley that night. So, in his mind in the town while he was yet on the hill, the farmer drew near to a place known as Thieves' Hole. And there the horse stood still and would answer neither spur nor rein. The spur and rein she understood, and her master's stern command, but the eyes that held her were stronger than all these.

3 In pairs, **analyse** the opening paragraphs to some fantasy stories on page 64. Categorize the openings and explain the strategies the writers use to show character and setting.
4 In pairs, **discuss** the following:
● Which openings did you like best and why?
● Could you visualize the characters and the setting?
● **Identify** the elements the openings have in common.

HOW DOES A WRITER 'GRAB' THE READER'S INTEREST?

Read these openings from fantasy stories.

Chapter 1: An unexpected party

In a hole in the ground there lived a hobbit. Not a nasty, dirty, wet hole, filled with the ends of worms and an oozy smell, nor yet a dry, bare, sandy hole with nothing in it to sit down on or to eat: it was a hobbit-hole, and that means comfort.

The Hobbit *by J. R. R. Tolkien*

The Legend of Alderley

At dawn one still October day in the long ago of the world, across the hill of Alderley, a farmer from Mobberley was riding to Macclesfield fair.

The Weirdstone of Brisingamen *by Alan Garner*

Chapter 1: The Shah of Blah

There was once in the country of Alifbay, a sad city, the saddest of cities, a city so ruinously sad that it had forgotten its name. It stood by a mournful sea full of glumfish, which were so miserable to eat that they made people belch with melancholy even though the skies were blue.

Haroun and the Sea of Stories *by Salman Rushdie*

Will tugged at his mother's hand and said, 'Come on, come on …'

But his mother hung back. She was still afraid. Will looked up and down the narrow street in the evening light, along the little terrace of houses, each behind its tiny garden and its box hedge, with the sun glaring off the windows of one side and leaving the other in shadow. There wasn't much time. People would be having their meal about now, and soon there would be other children around, to stare and comment and notice. It was dangerous to wait, but all he could do was persuade her, as usual …

The Subtle Knife *by Philip Pullman*

1.

Mrs. Whatsit

IT WAS A DARK AND STORMY NIGHT.

In her attic bedroom Margaret Murry, wrapped in an old patchwork quilt, sat on the foot of her bed and watched the trees tossing in the frenzied lashing of the wind. Behind the trees clouds scudded frantically across the sky. Every few moments the moon ripped through them, creating wraithlike shadows that raced along the ground.

The house shook.

Wrapped in her quilt, Meg shook.

A Wrinkle in Time *by Madeleine L'Engle*

Prologue

In an unremarkable room, in a nondescript building, a man sat working on very non-nondescript theories.

The man was surrounded by bright chemicals in bottles and flasks, charts and gauges, and piles of books like battlements around him.

Un Lun Dun by China Miéville

ACTIVITY: Create your own opening

■ ATL

- ■ Communication skills: Write for different purposes

1 Now it's your turn. In pairs, **explore** ideas for an adventure that involves two friends going to find something.
2 You are going to write the two opening paragraphs to your story. Review the elements that make a fantasy story (see page 62) and **select** the ones that you want to use in your opening paragraph. Remember to give an idea of the setting in your opening too.
3 Try to vary your vocabulary. Go to https://wordcounter.net and cut and paste your writing into the text field. Look at the keyword density box to see if you are overusing any words. If you are, use a thesaurus to find different words to use instead.
4 Share your paragraph with your classmates.

◆ Assessment opportunities

- ◆ In this activity you have practised skills that are assessed using Criterion B: Organizing, Criterion C: Producing text and Criterion D: Using language.

Grabbing the reader

Use these ideas to help you grab the reader's attention.

Writing an opening/setting the scene

- Introduce something intriguing, or difficult to explain or account for.
- Present a character and describe their strange behaviour.
- Start with a dramatic event or use a dramatic exclamation.
- Use a rhetorical question.
- Start with dialogue.

Introducing character

- Use dialogue and action to present your character.
- Show what a character is like through their thoughts and ideas.
- Give your character a unique name.
- Use powerful verbs for thoughts, actions and feelings.

ⓘ Did you know that …

… the word 'fantasy' comes from the Middle English *fantasie* and from the Greek *phantasia*?

Think back to some of the myths and legends you read about in Chapter 2. Can you **identify** any elements of fantasy in those stories? Is it possible that modern fantasy as a genre may have evolved from early myths and legends?

Find images of early **fantasy tales**. **Compare and contrast** modern fantasy stories and the images.

Characterization is a key element in fantasy novels. The main characters, also known as the **protagonist** and **antagonist**, have the most influence on the outcome of the story. The protagonist is the main character who is out to do good. The antagonist is the character or force that is against the protagonist and is basically evil.

Some characters are more important than others because they grow and develop with the plot and play a significant role in the story. These characters are called major characters. Minor characters, on the other hand, might not be the main focus of the story but are still important as they contribute to the development of the main characters.

ACTIVITY: Characterization

■ ATL

■ Communication skills: Negotiate ideas and knowledge with peers and teachers

1 Individually, write a brief paragraph about yourself. Include qualities you believe you have, your interests and anything else that would give an insight into who you are. Share your paragraph with a partner.
2 Discuss the idea of characters, morality (personal values) and what characteristics define someone.

◆ Assessment opportunities

◆ In this activity you have practised skills that are assessed using Criterion D: Using language.

ACTIVITY: The IB learner profile

■ ATL

■ Creative-thinking skills: Create original works and ideas; use existing works and ideas in new ways

■ The IB learner profile

1 In *The Weirdstone of Brisingamen*, consider Susan's or Colin's character. Which of the qualities of the IB learner profile does your chosen character have?
2 **Create** a poster for your character. Draw a picture of your character and surround the picture with these qualities. Support each quality with a relevant quote from the story and add an **explanation** of the quote and how it demonstrates the quality.

◆ Assessment opportunities

◆ In this activity, you have practised skills that are assessed using Criterion A: Analysing and Criterion C: Producing text.

▼ Links to: Individuals and societies: Geography

Developing a sense of place through the study of geography gives us a deeper understanding of national, European and global contexts.

How is your country divided? **Explore** the different regions in your country. **Select** a region and make notes on:

ACTIVITY: What is the *dramatis personae*?

■ ATL

- Communication skills: Preview and skim texts to build understanding

The Weirdstone of Brisingamen contains many characters, most of whom are magic or mystical in some way.

Dramatis personae is a Latin phrase that literally means 'person(s) of drama' (it is a plural noun but can be treated as singular or plural). It is a list of the main characters, and some of the lesser ones, in a book or play, with information about who they are, to whom they are related, and what they look like.

1 Having read *The Weirdstone of Brisingamen*, write a *dramatis personae*. Skim and scan through the book to check you have included the most important characters.
    Set out your character list with the character's name, followed by an **explanation** including: what the character or group of characters look like, who they are and any other information that you think will help others to understand the book.
2 Present your list to your classmates and give each other feedback.
3 In pairs or groups of three, **explore** the similarities and differences in the lists presented.

◆ Assessment opportunities

- In this activity you have practised skills that are assessed using Criterion A: Analysing.

- location and climate
- population and economy.

Add your own categories to the list above.

How is your country governed and who lives there?

ACTIVITY: Gowther Mossock

■ ATL

- Collaboration skills: Listen actively to other perspectives and ideas

Look at Chapter 1, 'Highmost Redmanhey', of *The Weirdstone of Brisingamen*.

1 In pairs, **discuss** the appearance and personality of Gowther Mossock. What sort of humour do you think he has? How do you know?
2 **Analyse** his dialect and accent. How does this add to your impression of the character?

◆ Assessment opportunities

- In this activity you have practised skills that are assessed using Criterion A: Analysing.

EXTENSION

In Chapter 1, we looked at Standard English and what it is (see page 8). Languages are evolving all the time and they differ according to place and social setting.

1 Use a search engine and find out about accents and dialects in the UK. Make notes and open up a file to record the sources you have used in your research as you go along.

2 Visit the sound map on this website to listen to other accents and dialects from the British Isles: **http://sounds.bl.uk/Sound-Maps/Accents-and-Dialects**.

3 Prepare a two-minute presentation on dialects and accents in the UK. Make sure you include your own definitions for dialect and accent.

4 Why not investigate speech in your community? How is language changing in your area? What is distinctive about speech in your area?

LANGUAGE IN CONTEXT

So far, we have focused on the features of the fantastic genre. But, it is impossible to study literature of any genre without considering the use of language. The language and stylistic choices made by fantasy writers allow us to immerse ourselves in 'realities' which are very different from our own. Language can be used to introduce character and setting but sometimes we need a little help to make sense of these strange and exotic landscapes and their inhabitants. Making comparisons with things that are familiar to us can make what is unreal and unfamiliar easier for us to understand.

ⓘ
- **Literal language** Literal means actual. Literal language describes something as it actually is. For example: *The grass is green*. A literal comparison will compare two things, focusing on real features. It is objective rather than subjective.
- **Figurative language** uses similes, metaphors, hyperbole and personification to describe something, often by comparing it with something else.
- **Impression or impressionistic language** refers to language that explains general feelings or thoughts rather than specific knowledge or facts.

ⓘ
hyperbole Exaggeration for effect, for example: *I've told you a thousand times.*

metaphor When an image is created by referring to something as something else, for example: *You're a star.*

simile A simile compares something to something else using 'like' or 'as', for example: *As big as a house.*

ACTIVITY: PEA paragraph

■ ATL

- ■ Communication skills: Read critically and for comprehension; use a variety of organizers for academic writing tasks

In pairs or groups of three, re-read Chapters 1 and 2 of *The Weirdstone of Brisingamen*, focusing in particular on extracts that describe the Edge.

1 **Comment** on the impression the Edge makes on Colin and Susan by copying and completing the table below.

	Example (quote)	Explanation/ Effect
Literal comparison		
Impressions		
Metaphor		
Simile		

2 After you have completed the table and discussed the quotes, choose *one* example and write a short PEA paragraph about it. Read the guidelines on how to write the perfect PEA (see page 69).

3 How effective is your PEA? Swap it with a partner and ask them to use various colours to highlight your paragraph to ensure that you've done the following:
   - Have they clearly established their point? Do you know from their topic sentence what the rest of the paragraph will be about?
   - Have they included quote/s?
   - Have they used relevant words, such as metaphor, simile, and so on?

4 Do the same for your partner's PEA.

◆ Assessment opportunities

- ◆ In this activity you have practised skills that are assessed using Criterion B: Organizing, Criterion C: Producing text and Criterion D: Using language.

How to write the perfect PEA

No, we're not talking about the small green vegetables you find on your plate at dinner time! A PEA paragraph is a useful way to structure your analysis of a particular quote or example.

The letters PEA stand for:

Point – This is what you want to get across. Start off by stating this clearly.

Evidence – This is usually a quote that you can use to support your point.

Analysis – This is the part where you explain or analyse your quote.

Let's take a look at an example PEA paragraph.

Eragon is a fantasy novel by writer Christopher Paolini. Here we will look at how he establishes setting in the extract below.

Before writing your PEA, it can be helpful to annotate your text, so you know exactly what you can include. For help with annotation, look back at Chapter 2 (page 34) to refresh your memory.

Although it is tempting, and as much as we would like to, we cannot include *everything* in our PEA paragraph. As you study literature more, you will be able to develop your paragraphs further, but for now we will focus on just one aspect. Let's go with beauty.

> The writer uses a variety of language and stylistic choices to establish the setting and atmosphere in the text. Adjectives such as 'silvery' and 'glistening', words that are commonly associated with jewels or precious metals, are used here to create a sense of the magical beauty of the landscape.

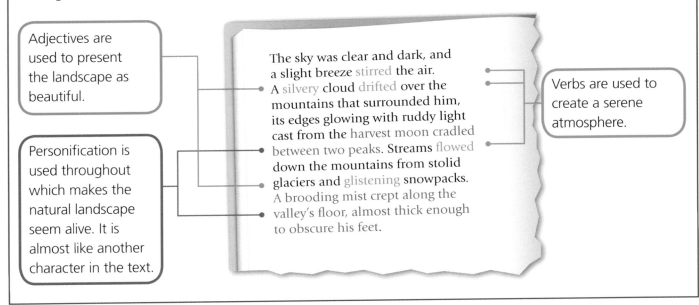

Adjectives are used to present the landscape as beautiful.

Personification is used throughout which makes the natural landscape seem alive. It is almost like another character in the text.

The sky was clear and dark, and a slight breeze stirred the air. A silvery cloud drifted over the mountains that surrounded him, its edges glowing with ruddy light cast from the harvest moon cradled between two peaks. Streams flowed down the mountains from stolid glaciers and glistening snowpacks. A brooding mist crept along the valley's floor, almost thick enough to obscure his feet.

Verbs are used to create a serene atmosphere.

ACTIVITY: Drawing Svarts

1 Read this description of the Svarts from *The Weirdstone of Brisingamen* and **identify** all the adjectives.
2 Now, draw an illustration of one or two of them using the description Alan Garner has written.

> They stood about three feet high and were man shaped, with thin, wiry bodies and limbs, and broad, flat feet and hands. Their heads were large, having pointed ears, round saucer eyes, and gaping mouths which showed teeth. Some had pug-noses, others thin snouts reaching to their chins. Their hides were generally of a fish-white colour, though some were black, and all were practically hairless.

3 In pairs, **compare and contrast** your illustrations. What are the similarities? In what ways do they differ? **Discuss** why the pictures might vary.
4 In pairs, **create** your own creature by writing a descriptive paragraph. **Select** carefully the adjectives you want to use. You may want to link this to the pieces of writing you have already completed during this chapter, or you can work on creating something new.

   Use a dictionary and thesaurus to help you find interesting words.
5 Swap your paragraphs with your classmates and draw an illustration. **Critique** your images with your classmates. Is the image for your paragraph how you had imagined it?

◆ Assessment opportunities

◆ In this activity you have practised skills that are assessed using Criterion C: Producing text and Criterion D: Using language.

Can we use fantasy to escape?

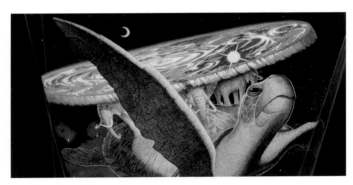

■ *Discworld* is Terry Pratchett's masterpiece in which characters float through space on the backs of four elephants, which in turn are standing on a giant turtle

■ A magical world created in the Discworld Emporium, in Wincanton, England

■ Author, Sir Terry Pratchett

Discworld is a series of fantasy novels written by the acclaimed British author, Terry Pratchett. The stories have been hugely successful and have been adapted for television, radio, theatre and film. You can even find video games and comic books based on the series.

Fantasy, possibly more so than other genres, appeals to people of all ages. Many of Pratchett's novels, which were originally intended for a younger audience, are popular with adults too. But this is not the first time we have witnessed this phenomenon; it's difficult to find someone who hasn't heard of Harry Potter, or indeed *The Lord of the Rings*, regardless of their age.

So, why are these stories so popular? Why do we plunge ourselves into unknown worlds, worlds occupied by wizards, trolls, elves, goblins and so many other remarkable creatures, time and time again? How can we link these fictional worlds to our own world and our own everyday experiences?

Perhaps it is in this gap between our world and the realm of fantasy where the secret lies. Fantasy fiction allows us to escape from the monotony of our everyday existence. In a world where we are constantly faced with trouble and strife, fantasy can be our saviour and through fiction we can find hope in far away, make-believe places, where good almost always triumphs over evil.

The power of magic has always intrigued us as humans and by reading fantasy stories we can indulge our fascination for it. Fantasy can make the ordinary extraordinary and we find ourselves believing, truly believing, in the worlds laid out before us by writers, even if it is just for a couple of hours at a time. These fantasy writers are themselves magicians of a kind – but their sorcery lies in their words not spells, and through their art they enchant us with their linguistic magic. But more on magic later …

There is more to fantasy than just escape. Fantasy teaches us to see things from other perspectives; to challenge our existing beliefs about the world; and to adopt a more open-minded way of looking at things. Fantasy teaches us that nothing is impossible if we put our minds and hearts into it.

Read the transcript below of Terry Pratchett in conversation with Dr Jacqueline Simpson, a researcher and author on folklore and legends.

Terry Pratchett: We've been not scathing, I think, about folklore, so I would like to ask you, what are the uses of folklore?

Jacqueline Simpson: To reconnect us with our past. To provide material for a lot of fun. To stimulate the imagination.

TP: Could I add one?

JS: Yes.

TP: To remind the kids that things were otherwise.

JS: Very true.

TP: That the human race did not pop out of the ground with iPods. That things were different. This is why I think a study of history is vital because as I always say, if you don't know where you've come from, you don't know where you are, and if you don't know where you are, you have no idea where you are going.

JS: I think that some themes that are found in folktales, perhaps more in the big fairy tales rather than the local stories, but still, some of these themes help us to understand ourselves, to understand our fears, to give courage and hope, don't you think?

TP: Yes, yes, but also to make life more fun, but not fun, satisfying.

JS: Yes, yes.

TP: I think actually one of the nice things about folklore is that it is in fact useless. It belongs to us, it doesn't cost anything, it changes, it moves, it disappears.

JS: And I may say that it is a delight to be a folklorist and to work on folklore because you never need worry whether the thing is true and accurate or not. As soon as you can prove that somebody has said it and somebody else has listened and repeated it, it doesn't matter a tinker's cuss whether it ever happened or not. Did King Alfred burn the cakes? Who the hell cares, the story's what matters.

ACTIVITY: Conversation with Terry Pratchett

■ ATL

- Communication skills: Make inferences and draw conclusions

Read the transcript of the conversation between Terry Pratchett and Dr Jacqueline Simpson.

In pairs or groups of three, discuss the following:

1 **What does Pratchett say about the purpose of folklore? Interpret what he means. What is your opinion about this?**

2 **Comment on what Dr Simpson says about truth and accuracy in folktales. What insight does this give us about fantasy and why it appeals to us as readers?**

◆ Assessment opportunities

- ◆ In this activity you have practised skills that are assessed using Criterion A: Analysing.

❶ Did you know ...

... that a set of writers created a group called the **Inklings** that met on Thursday evenings for readings, to exchange ideas and to give each other feedback on their own work?

Find out which writers belonged to this group, where they met and what connection they had besides a love of imaginative literature.

How can you identify a fantasy story?

We have already seen that every genre has a mixture of elements. But which elements in fantasy stories grab our attention the most? Which elements help us to escape into the depths of those unknown worlds?

The first would have to be magic! Magic is the basic ingredient of fantasy, whether it is Alice falling down a rabbit hole, Susan's tear or Platform 9¾ at King's Cross Station. Magic draws the reader in; the spells, the rituals, the supernatural – these elements form the backbone to the plot. We do not even question whether these things are possible as they are so deeply interwoven into the plot.

Another vital element in fantasy novels is **foreshadowing**. Foreshadowing is a technique that provides the reader with hidden clues to help us guess what might happen later in the story. It heightens our interest and encourages us to read more.

A **flashback** is an episode from the past that is inserted into the narrative. Sometimes the reader is aware of the event as it has already been revealed in the story. Alternatively, it can be about an event that has not been revealed to us, in which case it fills in gaps in the plot.

The plot is the sequence of events that applies to all fiction stories. Every story has a plot – it would not be a story without one. The four parts of a basic problem/resolution plot are:

- opening
- build-up
- dilemma events
- resolution.

Setting is the place and time in which a story happens, and is often important to a fantasy story. In fantasy, authors use invented settings, or imaginary worlds which bring their stories to life. The place can be as broad as Middle Earth from *The Lord of the Rings* or as specific as Hogwarts. The setting can (and usually does) change as the plot unravels. Usually the setting is revealed at the start of the story, along with the time frame or period. How many settings does *The Weirdstone of Brisingamen* have?

Guidelines for a literary circle

Role	Preparation	During discussion
Discussion director	Prepares between three and five key questions for the group to discuss. Look at the task to see what you need to focus on.	Leads the discussion, ensuring all members contribute and that the discussion stays on point.
Summarizer	Prepares a summary of the story or section of the novel the group is focusing on. Also gives feedback to the rest of the class once the task is completed.	Gives a summary of what the story is about, or recaps the last discussion and summarizes what has happened so far. This helps to focus the discussion.
Illustrator	Seeks out an image that represents the story or creates any form of visual that fits the purpose of the task.	Explains their choice of image and how it links to the text.
Vocabulary enricher	Selects certain words from the text – challenging words that they find definitions for, or interesting words that enrich the story.	Explains their choices and gives definitions.
Researcher	Finds background information on any relevant topic related to the book.	Presents information or material to the group to help understand the book better.
Connector	Finds connections between the story and real-life experiences based on the main themes in the story. Can also connect the book with other books they have read.	Explains why they made those connections and why they are relevant.

ACTIVITY: How can you identify a fantasy story?

A literature circle is a great way to engage in an open discussion about a book that you have read. As literature circles are independent reading groups, it is important for each member of the group to negotiate and decide on the role to take.

1 In groups of four or five, follow the guidelines on page 73 for how to set up a literature circle, and re-read *The Weirdstone of Brisingamen*.
2 In your literature group, look at the prompts below and choose between four and six that you want to focus on. For ideas on how to prepare further for your discussion visit: https://bit.ly/2MubvCb.
3 **Identify** examples of each of the literary elements listed in the table below by copying and completing the table.
4 Following your discussion, **summarize** your findings. **Justify** and present them to the rest of the class.

Literary element	Example
Magic	
Foreshadowing	
Flashback	
Plot	
Setting	
Time	

Prompts

1 **Identify** the most important characters in the story.
2 **Identify** the relationships of the characters to one another.
3 When and where does the story seem to take place? What clues in the story did you use to identify the place where (setting) and the time when the story took place?
4 Where does most of the action take place? Give examples of something that happened in each of the places you mention.
5 What part of the story was the most exciting? Unexpected? Surprising?
6 **Organize** the key events in the story.
7 **Summarize** the story.
8 **Interpret** the outcome of the story.
9 **Interpret** the author's purpose in writing the book. **Interpret** the main themes in the novel.
10 **Explain** the main character's actions in the story and describe how you might have acted differently. Think carefully about your decisions and **justify** your answer.
11 **Select** two characters in the story and **evaluate** who is the better of the two. **Justify** your choice.
12 Make a colourful illustration of an exciting scene in the book.
13 **Identify** a situation that happened to a character in the story and **comment** on whether you would have done the same thing he/she did or something different. What would you have done in that same situation?

ACTIVITY: Setting and real places

■ Map of a fantasy land filled with rivers, forests, mountains and castles

Old maps are fascinating because of the amount of detail they contain, the colours and the lettering. Fantasy books often contain maps. One of the most famous is the map in *The Lord of the Rings* of Middle Earth, which is a whole world created from the imagination of the author.

The Weirdstone of Brisingamen also starts with a map, but this map is different.

1 Read this article from the *Guardian* newspaper about the locations in the story. As you read, make notes about the locations and listen to the interview with Alan Garner:
https://bit.ly/3tisfwP.
- Why did Garner choose this setting for his story?
- **Evaluate** how the locations have changed.

- Is the map reliable?
- **Interpret** how the setting affects the action in the story.
- **Evaluate** the advantages of using a real setting for a story.
- **Interpret** how the setting makes you feel about the story.

2 In pairs, click on the Google maps link provided in the article and follow the trail. **Select** a few locations and search for the names of your chosen places. **Compare and contrast** the image with the description in the text.

3 Now it is your turn. In pairs or groups of three, **create** a setting. Remember that the setting of the story helps to determine what might happen and how we feel about what is happening.

4 Think about locations you know, that you have visited and find interesting. It could be your local area, a neighbourhood in your town or a place that you have visited. **Use** the prompts below to help you brainstorm ideas to describe your setting:
- What does the place look, sound and feel like?
- Where and when does the story take place?
- Use precise and realistic details.
- Which characters might live in your chosen setting?
- How does the setting make your character feel? Why?
- What are the challenges that might occur in the setting?

5 **Use** your notes and write a paragraph about the setting. Remember to appeal to at least three of the five senses in your description: taste, touch, sight, hearing and smell.

▼ Links to: Individuals and societies: History; Geography

Maps present information about the world in a simple, visual way. Nobody really knows how long maps have been around for, but map-like images have even been found in cave paintings. Carry out some research about the **history of cartography** and the ways that maps have influenced how we see and understand our world. How were maps made before satellites? How accurate were they?

Here is a good website with some tips on hand drawing shaded relief maps of mountainous areas: **www.reliefshading.com/examples**.

Watch the short animation *Try It!* on the website illustrating how detail is added to maps and then go to **www.fantasticmaps.com** for further tips.

In pairs or groups of three, **create** your own fantastic map to go with your setting.

Can you identify the book from its map? Test your knowledge here: **https://bit.ly/3tmGH6K**.

Look at Chapter 2 in *Individuals and Societies for the IB MYP by Concept 1* for more on maps.

Test your map reading skills. Follow the link below and have a go at playing the geography games: **https://bit.ly/3arOnvZ**.

ACTIVITY: Shake up your sentences

 ATL

- Reflection skills: (Re)considering the process of learning; choosing and using ATL skills; consider personal learning strategies; consider content

In pairs or groups of three, look back over some of the paragraphs you have written over the course of this chapter. See how many different sentence types you have used and discuss their effect.

Re-write some of your paragraphs, this time including as many different sentence types as you can.

◆ Assessment opportunities

- ◆ In this activity you have practised skills that are assessed using Criterion C: Producing text and Criterion D: Using language.

In Chapter 1 we looked at simple sentences. In your writing, you need to use a variety of sentences: simple, complex and compound.

Including a variety of sentences in your writing can make a huge difference on the effect your piece has on its audience. For example, you can add pace or create drama through the use of short sentences at an action-packed point in the narrative. Or you could use long, complex sentences to add more detailed description when you are establishing the setting in your story. Play around with your sentences and always aim to include as great a variety as you can.

Sentences

SIMPLE SENTENCE

The most basic type of sentence is the simple sentence, which contains only one clause.

A simple sentence can be as short as one word:

Melt!

Ice cream melts.

Ice cream melts quickly.

Ice cream melts quickly under the warm July sun.

COMPOUND SENTENCE

A compound sentence consists of two or more independent clauses (or simple sentences) joined by coordinating conjunctions such as *and*, *but* and *or*.

Simple sentence
India is a rich country.

It has many poor people.

Compound sentence
India is a rich country, but still it has many poor people.

COMPLEX SENTENCE

A complex sentence contains one independent clause and at least one dependent clause. Unlike a compound sentence, a complex sentence contains clauses which are not equal.

Simple sentences
My friend invited me to the cinema. I didn't want to go.

Compound sentence
My friend invited me to the cinema, but I didn't want to go.

Complex sentence
Although my friend invited me to the cinema, I didn't want to go.

! Take action: How can I make a difference?

! Fantasy stories often refer to displaced groups of people: characters who deal with personal challenges, difficult circumstances, conflict and other issues. For example, the dwarves in *The Hobbit*, or Charlie's family, who face hardship in *Charlie and the Chocolate Factory.*

! In groups, research a real-world example of one of the themes we have identified in a fantasy story. Present your example to your classmates and **evaluate** its relevance, inviting discussion from your peers.

! Compile your own anthology of fantastical stories from around the globe. Ask your peers to bring in an example of fantasy fiction and ask a teacher to help you create a booklet which you can photocopy and share. Ask your school librarian to keep a copy in the library to share with other members of your school community.

What does fantastic fiction reveal about the human imagination?

'We do not remember days, we remember moments. The richness of life lies in memories we have forgotten.' – Cesare Pavese, The Burning Brand: Diaries, 1935–1950

People are by nature inquisitive and explorers. Just think of all those moments of inspiration that led to so many amazing inventions. The process of invention relies on creativity, and an important part of this is recognizing creativity in the things around us. Familiarity means that we don't always do this, but considering the creative thinking behind an ordinary item like a pencil or something more abstract like a story can help us to understand the limitations of things, to question and to see how we can improve things. This is not only inspiring, but by looking at the purpose of things, how they work, and who their audiences are, we begin to understand them better.

Fantastical fiction enables us to use creativity to solve challenging problems. It allows us to question the *status quo* of our world and think about alternatives and solutions. The plots in the novels usually involve optimism, often combined with empathy in a fight against evil. We use our imagination as a force for good and to find answers to our questions and to highlight the essential truths of our modern world. How does fantasy promote the development of a moral identity? Which characters are typically the ones who experience an identity crisis? Morality is the ability to choose between right and wrong, and opt for good conduct and socially acceptable behaviour.

Fantasy is truly about the limitlessness of our imagination. So, let's get creative.

ACTIVITY: Creative hunt

■ ATL

- Critical-thinking skills: Draw reasonable conclusions and generalizations; consider ideas from multiple perspectives

Let's consider the book *The Weirdstone of Brisingamen* by Alan Garner from a creative viewpoint. Creative things have a purpose.

1 Look at the prompts below and **explore** the elements of creativity in this book. First, write down your ideas on sticky notes individually, then share with your classmates.
   - Identify the main purpose of the book.
   - Identify the different parts in the story.
   - Identify the audience.
   - Which parts of the story are the most creative? Try to rank them.
2 Go over your ranked lists and add more items. **Comment** on how this novel is creative, and **justify** your answer with examples.
3 Now choose an everyday object and use the same prompts. Think about what it's for and how it works and who its audience is. In pairs, **discuss** any part you think is particularly smart or creative.

◆ Assessment opportunities

- ◆ In this activity you have practised skills that are assessed using Criterion A: Analysing.

ⓘ A TED Talk is a platform for speakers to present great, well-informed ideas in under 18 minutes. It is run by the TED organization.

ACTIVITY: Build yourself a world

Creating worlds is one of the most important elements of fantasy. Have a go at creating your own world. Go back to your descriptive paragraph on setting and use your ideas as a starting point.

1 **Create** an adventurous quest story to go with your world. A quest is a journey where something needs to be found, returned to its rightful owner or protected so that it doesn't fall into the wrong hands. For example, in *The Weirdstone of Brisingamen*, Cadellin is desperate to find Firefrost.

2 **Follow** the link and the instructions to **create** your adventure: http://textadventures.co.uk/.

3 **Share** your game with your peers and take turns to write a review of your adventure games. Publish your reviews in your school newsletter or magazine and include a link so that other students can play your games.

◆ Assessment opportunities

◆ In this activity you have practised skills that are assessed using Criterion C: Producing text and Criterion D: Using language.

ACTIVITY: What fear can teach us

The American novelist Karen Thompson Walker begins her TED Talk by asking us to use our imagination and setting a scene:

> Imagine you're a shipwrecked sailor adrift in the enormous Pacific. You can choose one of three directions and save yourself and your shipmates – but each choice comes with a fearful consequence too. How do you choose?

1 In pairs, predict what the talk might be about.
2 Listen to her talk about 'fear' https://bit.ly/3rg4PX6 and consider the following:
   - **Identify** the author's purpose.
   - **Examine** the claim Karen makes about our relationship with fear.
   - **Interpret** how we are encouraged to think of fear.
   - **Evaluate** what might happen if we were to consider 'fear' in a new way.
   - **Comment** on how fear can be used as a tool in writing.
   - **Identify** the word the author suggests we use to substitute 'fear'.
   - What kind of writer is Karen?
   - According to the author, can our fears predict the future? How does she **justify** her point of view?
   - What's the title of the story?
   - **Outline** how the story of the sailors ends. Were you surprised by the outcome?
   - **Summarize** in two or three sentences the author's message about fear.
   - How do you feel about fear? What's your worst fear?
   - Do you agree or disagree with the author's point of view? Why? Why not?

◆ Assessment opportunities

◆ In this activity you have practised skills that are assessed using Criterion A: Analysing.

SOME SUMMATIVE TASKS TO TRY

Use these tasks to apply and extend your learning in this chapter. These tasks are designed so that you can evaluate your learning at different levels of achievement in the Language and literature criteria.

THIS TASK CAN BE USED TO EVALUATE YOUR LEARNING IN CRITERION B, CRITERION C AND CRITERION D

Task 1

Timing recommendation: 60 minutes

In this chapter you have read the novel *The Weirdstone of Brisingamen* and looked at excerpts from other fantasy stories.

For this task you will develop your writing skills by **creating** your own piece of fantasy literature.

Choose one of these prompts to write your story:

1 A stolen book and a sinister stranger.
2 A birthday party invitation and a locked cupboard.
3 A secret diary and something unexpected under the bed.

Remember, it's important to plan before writing. Take ten minutes to plan. Here are some pointers:

- Decide on your character(s). Think carefully about physical description, personality, background, motivation, and so on.
- Consider your setting. Where does the story take place? When does your story take place?
- Remember to think about all five senses when writing description.
- Make sure you have a strong plotline. Decide on a beginning, middle and end.

Susan's question was answered. They were in the middle of a ring of stones, and the surrounding low, dim shapes rose on the limit of vision as though marking the boundary of the world.

Facing the children were two stones, far bigger than the rest, and on one of the stones sat a figure, and the sight of it would have daunted a brave man.

For three fatal seconds the children stared, unable to think or move. And as they faltered, the jaws of the trap closed about them; like a myriad snakes, the grass within the circle, alive with the magic of the place, writhed about their feet, shackling them in a net of blade and root, tight as a vice.

As if in some dark dream, Colin and Susan strained to tear themselves free, but they were held like wasps in honey.

Slowly the figure rose from its seat and came towards them. Of human shape it was, though

- Choose a narrative voice and stick to it. Will you use the third or first person narrative voice?

THIS TASK CAN BE USED TO EVALUATE YOUR LEARNING IN CRITERION A

Task 2

Timing recommendation: 60 minutes

Read the extract above from *The Weirdstone of Brisingamen* by Alan Garner and answer these questions.

For each question make sure you include evidence from the text to support your response.

1 What do we learn about the setting in the extract?
2 **Identify** how Garner creates suspense in the opening lines.
3 What stylistic device does Garner use to show the difficulties faced by Colin and Susan in paragraph four? Why is it effective?
4 **Comment** on how the characters are developed in this extract. What do we learn about Colin and Susan? How is the mysterious 'figure' described?
5 Write **three** PEA paragraphs about how Alan Garner creates a sense of fear in the extract. Make sure you consider the use of language and stylistic devices.

like no mortal man, for it stood near eight feet high and was covered from head to foot in a loose habit, dank and green, and ill concealing the terrible thinness and spider strength of the body beneath. A deep cowl hid the face, skin mittens were in the wasted hands, and the air was laden with the reek of foul waters.

The creature stopped in front of Susan and held out a hand; not a word was spoken.

'No!' gasped Susan. 'You shan't have it!' And she put her arm behind her back.

'Leave her alone!' yelled Colin. 'If you touch her, Cadellin will **kill** you!'

The shrouded head turned slowly towards him, and he gazed into the cavern of the hood; courage melted from him, and his knees were water.

From The Weirdstone of Brisingamen,
Chapter 6: 'A Ring of Stones'

Reflection

In this chapter we explored the key narrative features of the fantasy genre, especially setting, character and theme. We have applied our newfound understanding of fantastical fiction to an extended study of Alan Garner's *The Weirdstone of Brisingamen: A Tale of Alderley* and had a go at creating fictional settings and characters of our own. Most significantly, we have learnt how the creativity and illimitable power of the human imagination can be expressed through literature.

Use this table to reflect on your own learning in this chapter.					
Questions we asked	Answers we found	Any further questions now?			
Factual: What is fantasy? How can you identify a fantasy story? How is fantasy different from other genres?					
Conceptual: What does fantastic fiction reveal about the human imagination? Can we use fantasy to escape? How does life in the fantasy world help us learn about the real world?					
Debatable: Why do we create? What does fantastic fiction reveal about the human imagination?					
Approaches to learning you used in this chapter:	Description – what new skills did you learn?	How well did you master the skills?			
		Novice	Learner	Practitioner	Expert
Collaboration skills					
Communication skills					
Creative-thinking skills					
Critical-thinking skills					
Information literacy skills					
Organization skills					
Reflection skills					
Learner profile attribute(s)	*Reflect on the importance of a thinker for your learning in this chapter.*				
Thinker					

4 Do advertisements run the world?

○ Advertisements share a common **purpose**, but through making certain linguistic and **stylistic choices**, writers can **communicate** ideas and tailor their **messages** to appeal to specific **audiences** on a **global** scale.

CONSIDER THESE QUESTIONS:

Factual: What is an advertisement? Are there different types of adverts?

Conceptual: What is the purpose of advertising? How do advertisers use language to appeal to certain audiences? What can we learn about people and society through adverts? How has advertising changed over time?

Debatable: Can advertising be dangerous? Does advertising influence the way we think?

Now **share and compare** your thoughts and ideas with your partner, or with the whole class.

○ IN THIS CHAPTER, WE WILL ...

■ **Find out** what advertisements are.
■ **Explore** the impact that advertising has on our behaviour and way of thinking.
■ **Take action** to raise awareness about the dangerous consequences of irresponsible advertising.

■ These Approaches to Learning (ATL) skills will be useful ...

■ Communication skills
■ Creative-thinking skills
■ Critical-thinking skills
■ Information literacy skills
■ Media literacy skills

◆ Assessment opportunities in this chapter:

◆ **Criterion A:** Analysing
◆ **Criterion B:** Organizing
◆ **Criterion C:** Producing text
◆ **Criterion D:** Using language

We will reflect on this learner profile attribute …

- Communicators – we express ourselves confidently and creatively in many ways.

KEY WORDS

advertising	charity	marketing
brand	logo	slogan
commercial	public service	

We don't need to travel far to come face to face with an advertisement. They're everywhere, and we are constantly bombarded by words and images enticing us to buy, to spend, to consume.

Adverts are all around us. They stare down upon us, projected on high-rise buildings or plastered on billboards of gigantic proportions; or they might glare at us from the sides of buses and taxis. They are spread out across the pages of magazines; they sneak their way into the columns of newspapers or pop up on our screens as we browse the internet. They are in our classrooms, in our shopping centres, in our streets; we find them pinned on the noticeboards in the waiting rooms of doctors' surgeries and dental practices. Adverts have even found their way into our homes; they peer out at us from our kitchen cupboards and filter into our living rooms through our televisions and radios. We cannot escape them.

DISCUSS

When was the last time you purchased something after seeing or a hearing an advertisement?

1   In pairs or groups of three, **discuss** your last advert-inspired purchase. If you can, find the advert.
2   Consider the following questions:
  - Where did you come across the advert? Was it in a magazine? Did you see it on a billboard? Online? On television? Perhaps you heard it on the radio?
  - What was the product and did you know anything about it before seeing/hearing the advert?
  - What was it about the advert that convinced you to buy the item? Why did the advert or product appeal to you in particular?
  - What expectations did you have after seeing/hearing the advert? Did the product live up to these expectations or were you disappointed?
3   Now, on your own, consider the following question:
  - Are you influenced by advertisements?

  Give yourself a score between 0 (not influenced) and 10 (easily influenced), and write this on a sticky note. We will reflect on this at the end of the chapter.

What is an advertisement?

WHERE CAN WE FIND ADVERTISEMENTS?

What is advertising and why are we surrounded by advertisements? Advertisements, or as they are commonly known in their abbreviated form, adverts or ads, are generally used to describe or draw attention to a product, service or event. This can be anything from an item of clothing or a loan, to a television programme or a music festival. The main purpose of an advertisement is to persuade consumers to invest in an idea or a product but an advert often serves a secondary purpose, which is to provide information.

The message of an advert is incredibly important and to ensure that this is conveyed effectively, advertisements are carefully constructed by making language and stylistic choices.

In this chapter we will consider the ever-changing face of advertising and its seemingly limitless power to influence our ideas and habits.

ACTIVITY: Advert anthology

■ ATL

- Media literacy skills: Locate, organize, analyse, evaluate, synthesize and ethically use information from a variety of sources and media
- Information literacy skills: Evaluate and select information sources and digital tools based on their appropriateness to specific tasks

Let's investigate how frequently we come across adverts in our daily lives.

1 Keep a record of how many advertisements you see or hear over the course of one day. For each advert:
   - Note down where you saw the advert. Be as specific as possible.
   - Identify the *purpose* of the advert – what is it trying to persuade you to do?
   - Synthesize the *message* of the advert.
   - Identify the target *audience*.
   - Reflect on how you felt after seeing the advert. Did it influence you in anyway?
2 Discuss your findings with your class.
3 Now, compile an advert anthology to use later on in this chapter – aim to find at least ten printed adverts. Don't forget to make a note of where you found them.

◆ Assessment opportunities

- In this activity you have practised skills that are assessed using Criterion A: Analysing and Criterion B: Organizing.

What is the purpose of advertising?

Advertisements come in all shapes and forms and while they may have different messages to convey, they share a common purpose – to persuade. That could mean getting you to buy a product, convincing you to donate money to a worthwhile cause or encouraging you to change your behaviour or attitude about a particular social issue.

We have already seen that adverts can be transmitted in all sorts of mediums including television, print, radio and online. Now let's look at the types of advertisements we are exposed to.

- On hearing the word 'advertisement', many of us automatically think of the adverts which appear on our television screens, either persuading us to buy a certain product or to watch another television programme. These are called **commercial advertisements** and are used by companies to promote their products or services so that they can make a financial profit.
- But adverts can be used for more noble reasons, such as fundraising for worthwhile causes. Adverts that persuade you to donate money to charitable organizations are called **charity advertisements**. In this case, the charity does not make a profit. Instead, some of the money made as a result of the campaign goes to a specific cause – whether that be medical research or responding to a humanitarian crisis. The rest is used to cover the charity's costs so that they can continue campaigning in future.
- Some advertisements don't require you to spend money on a product or donate money, but instead raise awareness of issues that may affect public health or safety. These are known as **public service advertisements** or announcements. They are usually used by government organizations to invite audiences to reflect on their behaviour, actions or lifestyle choices and make changes for the better.

ⓘ Did you know that ...

... the first advertisement to be broadcast on television was for Bulova watches in 1941 in the United States?

... the first adverts can be traced back to the ancient Egyptians? Apparently, they used papyrus to make sales messages and posters.

Use the internet to find out more about the **history of advertising**.

Sentence moods

In English, there are four sentence moods which help us identify the purpose of the sentence.

- **Declarative** – These sentences make statements or 'declare' things and always end in a full stop. For example: *This is a car.*
- **Exclamatory** – These sentences end with an exclamation mark and are used to express strong feelings. For example: *I'm so excited!*
- **Interrogative** – These sentences end with a question mark and are used to ask questions or make requests. For example: *Where am I?*
- **Imperative** – Like declarative sentences, these sentences also end in a full stop but they are used to give instructions or commands. For example: *Stop writing.*

DISCUSS

In pairs or groups, **discuss** which sentence moods you are most likely to find in advertisements. Can you think of some reasons why?

ACTIVITY: What makes an advertisement?

■ ATL

- ■ Communication skills: Read critically and for comprehension

Advertisements are carefully crafted in order to achieve the desired effect on their audience.

Let's look more closely at some advertisements and consider some of the **stylistic choices** made by advertisers to persuade their audiences to buy, donate or make a change to their lifestyle.

In pairs, explore the advertisements on pages 87–89 and answer the following questions:

1 Other than purpose, what do the advertisements have in common? Can you **identify** any stylistic features that appear in more than one of the adverts?
2 Who is the target audience for each advertisement?
3 What is the message of each advertisement?
4 Adverts that appear in magazines contain more written content than poster advertisements. Why do you think this is?

◆ Assessment opportunities

- ◆ In this activity you have practised skills that are assessed using Criterion A: Analysing.

Language and Literature for the IB MYP 1: *by Concept*

Let's look at some different types of adverts.

COMMERCIAL ADVERT – MAGAZINE

WHOLESOME. HAVE SOME.

Alliteration The use of **alliteration** creates a soft tone and emphasizes the word 'wholesome' – one of many **adjectives** used to describe the product. Find some more examples of adjectives used in the advert and consider their effect.

Parallelism Parallelism is the repetition of a phrase or grammatical structure. Why do you think the advertisers have made this stylistic choice? What effect does it create? How does it help convey the message of the advert?

Listing The listing of nouns gives information to the audience. Can you find any other examples in the text?

Direct address – second person pronouns What is the effect of **directly addressing** the audience? What does it suggest about the organization?

Not only are McDonald's meals good to eat, they're good for you.

Bread, meat, milk and potatoes. These foods form the basis of the essential food groups recommended by the Commonwealth Dept. of Health for a well-balanced, nutritious diet. That's what we sell at McDonald's.

Our buns are made from top quality, enriched Australian wheat flour, baked locally and delivered fresh.

The meat in a McDonald's burger is top quality, lean, Australian beef. It includes selected cuts of rump, round, topside and sirloin.

There are no fillers. No cereals. No chemical additives. No tenderizers. Nothing artificial. Just pure, 100% Australian beef.

Our rich, thick Shakes are made from real fresh dairy milk.

Our world-famous French Fries are made from real Tasmanian grown potatoes.

Have some wholesome McDonald's meals and you're on your way to a well-balanced diet.

Nutritional Analysis conducted by independent Australian laboratory.
Analysis available on request by writing to McDonald's Restaurants, 231 Miller Street, North Sydney, N.S.W. 2060.

McD3680/81

Facts and statistics, expert opinion Why might the company include these? Why might they persuade the audience to buy the product?

CHARITY ADVERT – POSTER

Emotive language What kind of feelings do you think this **emotive language** will produce? Why might they encourage audiences to donate?

Inclusive personal pronouns Using **inclusive pronouns** makes the audience feel more involved in the campaign and forces them to take responsibility.

Imperative sentences What is the effect of these? Can you find any imperative sentences in the previous advert?

Rhyme Rhyming is often used in adverts to make the message more memorable. In this case, the words of an existing nursery rhyme have been changed to highlight the fact that the girls in the poster miss out on their childhood. Why might this be an effective stylistic choice?

Torture and strain and backbreaking pain, That's what little girls are made for.

Your donation to WaterAid will be **doubled** by the UK Government

Direct address

Girls are made for more than this.

Give girls the future we'd want for our sisters and daughters. Every pound you donate before 9th September **will be doubled**, reaching twice as many girls with clean water.

Facts

Visit wateraid.org/uk/girlscampaign2014 **or call** 020 7793 4594

TO BE A GIRL

Matching your donations with UKaid

WaterAid

Registered charity numbers 288701 (England and Wales) and SC039479 (Scotland)

WaterAid/Abbie Trayler-Smith

PUBLIC SERVICE ADVERT – POSTER

Exclamatory sentences
Why do you think the advertisers have used an exclamatory sentence? What is the effect?

Can you identify any examples of **humour** used in the text? Who do you think the target audience might be? How might humour make the poster more appealing to them?

Inclusive pronouns

Emotive language
What effect might these words have on the audience?

Facts and statistics

Discourse marker and fronted conjunctions
to create a more conversational tone. How might this help engage the audience?

Imperative sentences

Presentational devices

Creating printed advertisements involves not only making language and stylistic choices, but also using **presentational devices**. These are features that help to enhance the **message** the advert is trying to convey and can help to present information to the **audience** in an engaging and accessible way.

Here are some of the presentational devices commonly found in advertisements:

- **Images:** This includes both photographs and illustrations. Images are used to visually engage a reader's interest but can also be used to influence their point of view. Sometimes an image is accompanied by a **caption**, a brief explanation or comment. We consider two things when we look at an image: the **denotation**, what it is actually showing us; and, more importantly, the **connotations**, which is what the picture implies, or the ideas or feelings the advertiser wants the audience to associate the image with.
- **Logos and slogans:** Logos are especially important in advertising because they are a visual representation of an organization's identity or brand. A slogan is a short, catchy phrase, which can make an advert's message more memorable to the audience.
- **Colour:** We all interpret things differently, but for many of us a specific colour carries certain associations; for example, the colour red is often associated with danger, passion or anger, depending on the context. This can vary from culture to culture. Advertisers can use colours to evoke certain feelings in their audience. Can you think of any other colours that have strong associations with certain moods or feelings?
- **Charts and diagrams:** If you are giving your audience lots of facts and statistics, it might be a good idea to present your information in a clear and simple format that they can easily understand. Graphs, pie charts and timelines are often used in advertisements for this reason.
- **Font styles:** Thinking carefully about the font used in an advert can really pay off. A particular font style or typeface can be used to draw attention to a specific point, or to differentiate between ideas. Fonts can also influence the mood or tone of a text.

ACTIVITY: Presentational devices

ATL

- Communication skills: Make inferences and draw conclusions; organize and depict information logically
- Media literacy skills: Understand the impact of media representations and modes of presentation; compare, contrast and draw connections among (multi)media resources
- Critical-thinking skills: Gather and organize relevant information to formulate an argument

Look again at the three advertisements on pages 87–89.

1 **Copy and complete the table below. For each presentational device, consider the impact it might have on the audience.**

Presentational device	Commercial advert	Charity advert	Public service advert
Images			
Logos and slogans			
Colour			
Charts and diagrams			
Font styles			

Language and Literature for the IB MYP 1: *by Concept*

ACTIVITY: Create your own advert

Now that we know a little bit more about the conventions of advertisements, let's have a go at creating our own.

1 In groups of three, brainstorm some ideas about the kind of advert you'd like to make.
Use the following questions to help you plan:
 • What kind of advert is it going to be? Charity? Commercial? Public service?
 • What format will your advert take? Is it for a magazine or newspaper? Is it to appear online? Is it a poster? If so, where should it be displayed?
 • What **message** do you want to get across?
 • Who is your target audience?
 • How will you engage your audience? Think about language, stylistic choices and presentational devices.

2 As a group, negotiate ideas and agree on the resources you want to use and then start to work on putting your advert together.
3 Once you've finished, swap your advertisement with another group and **annotate** their advert to **identify** the language, stylistic features and presentational devices they have included.
 Have they missed anything? How effective is their advert? Give each other some feedback.
4 To finish, write a PEA paragraph that compares your advert and the one you have annotated. Focus on one of the following, which is used in both adverts:
 • A presentational device
 • A stylistic feature
In your paragraph, you should **evaluate** the potential impact of your selected feature on the intended audience.

2 On a copy of each advert, **annotate** the presentational devices in mind. **Discuss** how the presentational devices help to get the message of each advert across.
3 **Evaluate** which advert makes the best use of presentational devices.

EXTENSION

Choose two of the adverts from your advert anthology. Can you **identify** any presentational devices? **Comment** on the effect of each one.

How do advertisers use language to appeal to certain audiences?

Awareness of the audience is hugely important in advertising. In order to ensure that they get the desired response, advertisers tailor their adverts to the needs of their specific target audience by making careful language and stylistic choices. Advertising companies often carry out extensive market research to give them a detailed understanding of their audience.

For instance, teenagers and young people are more likely to respond to adverts that mirror their way of speaking. This can include the use of colloquial language common to their age group, and a lively and conversational tone. Linguists have found that men and women respond differently to certain words and phrases and use language differently. To give you an example, women tend to use more specific colour terms than men, as illustrated in this humorous colour chart: **https://bit.ly/2YEsgNA**.

In this section, we'll look at some examples that illustrate the way in which advertisers use language to convey certain messages to specific audiences.

ACTIVITY: Seducing the buyer

ATL

- Creative-thinking skills: Create original works and ideas; use existing works and ideas in new ways
- Communication skills: Give and receive meaningful feedback

■ Isla Fisher plays the shopaholic in the film *Confessions of a Shopaholic*

Who doesn't like nice new things? We all like to indulge in some retail therapy once in a while. The retail industry can only survive if buyers like us continue buying so it has to find ways to get us to part with our money.

Confessions of a Shopaholic is a film based on a series of books of the same name by Sophie Kinsella. The story follows Rebecca Bloomwood, a self-confessed shopping addict, who gets herself into serious debt because of her uncontrolled spending.

1 **Watch a short clip from the film: https://youtu.be/xfPuQLbnsu8.**
   You'll notice that the mannequin has been personified, and successfully convinces Rebecca to do what she does best – shop!
2 **In pairs or groups of three, discuss the strategies the mannequin uses to convince Rebecca to buy the green scarf.**
3 **Now, on your own, imagine you are a product in a store – you might be a new pair of shoes, a guitar, a computer game, a book or an item of clothing.**
   You must convince someone to buy you. Write a short speech (100–150 words should be sufficient) using some of the techniques you've identified in the video. Make sure you describe your most appealing traits. Think about your audience – what will your potential buyer be like? What would attract them to you?
   Keep your product choice a secret and try not to reveal what you are in your piece of writing (for example, *don't* say 'I'm a pair of shoes').
4 **Read your speech to your peers and see if they can guess what you are. Ask them to give you some feedback so you can evaluate the effectiveness of your writing.**

◆ Assessment opportunities

◆ In this activity you have practised skills that are assessed using Criterion C: Producing text.

If you buy this product, your life will be better!

First conditional

Advertisers frequently use the **first conditional** to persuade their audiences to buy a product, or to donate money to a cause. It can also be used to warn audiences of the consequences of not buying into an idea or product. It's a way to make a deal of sorts with the audience, and to make them feel that their actions can have a positive, or sometimes negative, influence on a situation.

The first conditional is used to talk about things that are likely to happen in the future, based on a possible action in the present.

If + simple present, simple future

For example:

If it rains today, you will get wet.

If you don't hurry, you'll miss the train.

Let's consider the effect of using the first conditional in this advert.

Here, the advert uses the first conditional to challenge the audience to find the advertised product cheaper elsewhere. The challenge is a boast, as the company is confident that this will not happen but, if it does, they also promise to match the cheaper price.

A conditional is gentler than an **imperative**, but can be as effective in getting people to buy or donate to a cause.

ACTIVITY: Audience is everything

■ **ATL**

- Communication skills: Read critically and for comprehension
- Critical-thinking skills: Evaluate evidence and arguments

Look at the advertisements on pages 96 and 97 and complete the following tasks.

1 Taking into consideration the language used in each advert, which ones do you think are intended for teenagers, which for women and which for men?
2 For each advertisement, **identify the language** the advertisers have used in order to appeal to the target audience and **analyse the effect**.
3 Identify the **message** being conveyed in each advert. How does the language used help to get this message across?
4 **Evaluate** the role that presentational features play in each advert. What do you notice?
5 Consider whether the messages conveyed by any of the adverts are problematic. Do they play on stereotypes? **Discuss** in pairs or groups of three.

◆ Assessment opportunities

- In this activity you have practised skills that are assessed using Criterion A: Analysing.

EXTENSION

Choose two or three of the adverts from your advert anthology and **identify** the target audience. In pairs or groups of three:

- **Identify** the language and stylistic choices made by the writer to appeal to a specific audience.
- **Analyse** the effect of the language and stylistic choices and consider their impact on the audience.

ACTIVITY: Slogans

■ **ATL**

- Communication skills: Give and receive meaningful feedback

How can you make your adverts or brand more memorable? A slogan is the answer. Short, catchy and impossible to get out of your head, slogans have been used by advertisers for decades.

1 In pairs, **identify** the organization or product with which the following slogans are associated.
   - Just do it
   - Because I'm worth it
   - I'm lovin' it
   - Where do you want to go today?
   - It's the real thing
   - Finger lickin' good
   - Hello moto
2 Did you get all of them? If not, use a search engine to find out where they are from.
3 **Discuss** what you think makes a good slogan.
4 Now have a go at writing your own:
   - As a group, decide on a product – it can be something that exists already or you can invent something new.
   - On your own, write a slogan for your chosen product and share with the group.
   - As a group, **evaluate** which slogan is the best one for the product. Make sure you can **justify** your choice.

◆ Assessment opportunities

- In this activity you have practised skills that are assessed using Criterion C: Producing text.

Sooner or later, your wife will drive home one of the best reasons for owning a Volkswagen.

Women are soft and gentle, but they hit things.

If your wife hits something in a Volkswagen, it doesn't hurt you very much.

VW parts are easy to replace. And cheap. A fender comes off without dismantling half the car. A new one goes on with just ten bolts. For $24.95* plus labor.

And a VW dealer always has the kind of fender you need. Because that's the one kind he has.

Most other VW parts are interchangeable too. Inside and out. Which means your wife isn't limited to fender smashing.

She can jab the hood. Graze the door. Or bump off the bumper.

It may make you furious, but it won't make you poor.

So when your wife goes window-shopping in a Volkswagen, don't worry.

You can conveniently replace anything she uses to stop the car.

Even the brakes.

You'll be tickled pink

NOT AVAILABLE IN PINK.

YORKIE Nestlé

IT'S NOT FOR GIRLS

www.nestle.co.uk

■ The gender divide in advertising

What can we learn about people and society through adverts?

HOW HAS ADVERTISING CHANGED OVER TIME?

The advertisements from a particular place or period in history provide us with a valuable insight into the needs, wants, anxieties and even moral and social values of the audiences for which they are intended. Through adverts we can map the changes that societies have undergone over time, and also track human achievement through innovations and inventions that have made life easier for many of us.

Take, for example, the increase in the number of advertisements for white goods – refrigerators, ovens, washing machines – when they became more widely available in the 1950s. These adverts suggest that being able to own such appliances was considered a mark of success and affluence. But they also reflect contemporary views about the role of women in society as homemaker or housewife. Do you think advertisements today reflect how men's and women's roles have changed over the decades?

Each passing decade brings a new mindset and advertisers must continuously adapt the language and techniques used in their adverts in order to keep up with the demands of their ever-evolving audiences.

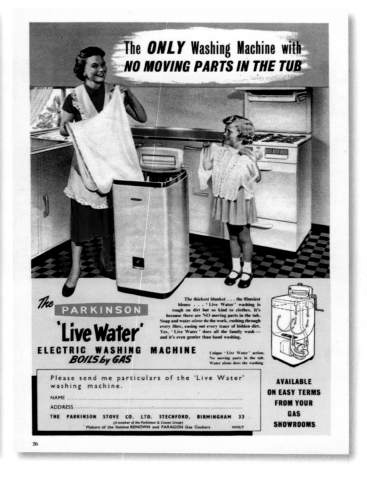

■ Adverts from the 1950s

ACTIVITY: Adverts around the world

Advertising is a global phenomenon and it's worth looking at advertising and attitudes towards advertising from around the world. What can we learn about the wishes, the fears and values of a country from their adverts?

Let's carry out some research:

1 **In pairs, choose a country and carry out a brief investigation about advertising there.**

2 You might want to focus on one particular advert, or how a particular product is advertised in your country of choice.
3 Find out which products are advertised the most and what this reveals about the country.
4 Consider how these adverts **compare** to adverts from other parts the world.
5 Your adverts can take any form – but you must be able to share them with your peers.
6 Prepare a short presentation for your class on your chosen place. You can present this in the form of a poster or by creating a slideshow on your computer.

ACTIVITY: Adverts past and present

Look at the adverts about smoking on pages 100–101.

1 For each one, in pairs or groups of three:
   • **Identify** whether they are commercial, charity or public service adverts.
   • **Identify** the specific purpose of each text. What are the similarities and how do they differ from one another?
   • **Explain** who the intended audience is for each advert. Support your answer using examples of language from the text.
   • **Discuss** the creator's choice of images in the adverts and the intended effect.
   • **Analyse** the effect of some of the language and stylistic choices made in each text.
   • **Discuss** what each advert reveals about attitudes to smoking. Have these attitudes changed over time?

2 Using PEA paragraphs, choose two of the adverts, and **compare** them. Make sure you include examples to support your ideas.

Adverts can be incredibly revealing and, through comparing adverts from bygone eras with those of today, we can see how much, or how little, attitudes surrounding certain issues have changed over time.

Look at the following adverts about smoking.

■ Advert for Lucky Strike cigarettes

■ Advert from the NHS, the National Health Service in the UK

■ Advert for Camel cigarettes

An advert for electronic cigarettes

EXTENSION: TIMELINE

Create an advertisement timeline for one of the following products:

- toys
- clothes
- beauty products or toiletries
- food.

To make things easier, you might want to focus on tracing the advertising history of a particular branded product. Find out:

- When the adverts for your product first appeared.
- How the advertisers adapted their use of language and stylistic choices over time.
- How the advent of new technology (TV, radio, internet) affected the advertising.

▼ Links to: Visual art

Look at the advert for Pears Soap, a product still widely available today. Isn't it beautiful? It was painted by the British artist John Everett Millais in 1886, and the little boy in the painting is his grandson William.

The painting was spotted in a newspaper by the managing director of A&F Pears, Thomas J Barratt, and he purchased the painting so that he could use it for the purpose of advertising.

Millais, who was by then one of the most popular artists in Britain, had some initial reservations about his art being used to promote the sales of soap. He couldn't really do anything about this, however, as Barratt owned the copyright to the picture. Some say that Millais eventually came around to the idea – despite being criticized by many people for 'selling out'.

What do you think appealed to Barratt about Millais' painting? Do you know of any other paintings that have been used for advertising?

Can advertising be dangerous?

DOES ADVERTISING INFLUENCE THE WAY WE THINK?

The power of advertisements extends beyond just influencing our consumer habits – adverts can also have a profound impact on the way we think about the world and ourselves. In the case of charity adverts and public service announcements, this influence is a largely positive one, but in the world of commercial advertising, lurking beneath the quirky slogans and bright images, there can be a worryingly negative message.

Advertising can be dangerous. Just think back to the smoking adverts from the early to mid twentieth century we have looked at in this chapter. These adverts presented smoking as glamorous and misled audiences into believing that smoking was good for you, something we now know to be completely untrue. Today, in some countries, cigarette packaging must carry a clearly visible health warning about the dangerous effects of smoking. Should cigarettes ever have been advertised if they cause such harm?

EXTENSION

Look back at your advert anthology. Do you think any of the adverts have a potentially dangerous or negative message? **Explain** why you think this and **discuss** in pairs or groups of three.

THINK-PAIR-SHARE

Read the statements below. Comment on them and record your response in three sentences.

- **Advertisements can have a negative impact on young people's ideas about self image.**
- **Advertisements can be responsible for health problems.**
- **Advertisements can lead to financial problems.**

Now, in pairs, share your sentences and discuss the statements. Make sure you are able to justify your comments.

ACTIVITY: Who should take responsibility?

■ ATL

- Media literacy skills: Understand the impact of media representations and modes of presentation
- Creative-thinking skills: Create original works and ideas; use existing works and ideas in new ways

To begin, watch this short compilation of television adverts which are aimed at children and teenagers: https://youtu.be/xk_hkdGf1tc.

1 As you watch, make notes with the following questions in mind:
    - What do they all have in common?
    - What is the message of each advert?
    - How many of the products advertised would you consider 'healthy'?
    - How many celebrities can you spot? Celebrity endorsement is the use of a famous person in an advertising campaign to promote a certain brand or product. What do you think the advantage of this might be for the advertisers?
    - Although in some countries there are bans on junk food advertising during television programmes aimed at young people, children and teenagers are still exposed to adverts promoting food products like the ones in the clip. What do you think the long- and short-term consequences of this might be? Is this dangerous?
    - Who should take responsibility for the problems that may potentially arise as a result of advertising? Is it the advertisers themselves? Or the celebrities who endorse such products?
2 In pairs or groups of three, **create** a public service advert to encourage young people to be more aware of the nutritional value of what they eat and not be persuaded by advertising.
3 Present your advert as a poster and display this in your classroom, or around your school.

◆ Assessment opportunities

- In this activity you have practised skills that are assessed using Criterion C: Producing text and Criterion D: Using language.

! Take action: How can I make a difference?

! While a great deal of good can come from advertising, we have to take action against irresponsible advertisements that can cause harm to us and others.

- **Call out irresponsible advertising!** Have you seen an advert that you feel is dangerous or unethical? Write to the publication, television network or the company that has produced the advert and express how you feel. Persuade them to remove the advert or rethink their campaign.

- **Reach out to celebrities:** Has a pop-star or actor that you admire been involved in a campaign that you feel could have a negative impact on young people? Write a letter reminding them about the responsibility they have as role models.

- Learn more about what advertisers can and cannot get away with by doing some research on how advertising is regulated in your country. In the United Kingdom it is an organization called the ASA. You can follow the link below to learn about what they do. **https://bit.ly/3bKNjVZ**

! On a more positive note, you can **apply** some of the skills you've learnt in this chapter to …

- **Create** posters to display in your school to raise awareness about certain causes and events.

A SUMMATIVE TASK TO TRY

Use this task to apply and extend your learning in this chapter. The task is designed so that you can evaluate your learning at different levels of achievement in the Language and literature criteria.

THIS TASK CAN BE USED TO EVALUATE YOUR LEARNING IN CRITERION A, CRITERION C AND CRITERION D

Look at the charity advert below. Make a copy of it and take some time to **annotate** it with language, stylistic choices and presentational devices in mind.

After you've annotated the poster, answer the following question:

How does the charity organization persuade the audience to support the cause?

Use PEA paragraphs to structure your response. You have 60 minutes to complete this task.

Reflection

In this chapter we have developed an understanding of what advertisements are and the **purpose** they serve – to persuade. We have also explored how advertisers **communicate** specific **messages** to certain target **audiences** through language and by making certain **stylistic choices**. We have learnt about the devices used in adverts and have had a go at creating our own. We have also considered the power of advertising to influence the way we think and behave, and have raised awareness about the dangers of irresponsible advertising.

Use this table to reflect on your own learning in this chapter.					
Questions we asked	Answers we found	Any further questions now?			
Factual: What is an advertisement? Are there different types of adverts?					
Conceptual: What is the purpose of advertising? How do advertisers use language to appeal to certain audiences? What can we learn about people and society through adverts? How has advertising changed over time?					
Debatable: Can advertising be dangerous? Does advertising influence the way we think?					
Approaches to learning you used in this chapter:	Description – what new skills did you learn?	How well did you master the skills?			
		Novice	Learner	Practitioner	Expert
Communication skills					
Creative-thinking skills					
Critical-thinking skills					
Information literacy skills					
Media literacy skills					
Learner profile attribute(s)	*Reflect on the importance of being a communicator for your learning in this chapter.*				
Communicator					

5 Is this for real?

○ Relationships between fictional **characters** guide the reader to **interpret a theme** and make **text-to-world** connections.

'It's sad that bad things have to happen in order for us to stop and look around.' – Megan Duke, Infinite Limits: A Conclusion to Small Circles

CONSIDER THESE QUESTIONS:

You will notice that this chapter is different. There are no factual, conceptual or debatable questions listed. See page 123 for the Activity.

○ IN THIS CHAPTER, WE WILL ...

- **Find out** how realistic fiction can raise awareness of issues that are far too often 'hidden'.
- **Explore** a realistic fiction novel, which is about people, their problems and the challenges they face, and consider how the characters' language and behaviour reflect the social and cultural aspects of the setting of the story.
- **Take action** to foster a more open-minded attitude towards the issues explored in realistic fiction and to offer support to those experiencing them.

◆ Assessment opportunities in this chapter:

- **Criterion A:** Analysing
- **Criterion B:** Organizing
- **Criterion C:** Producing text
- **Criterion D:** Using language

● We will reflect on this learner profile attribute …

- Caring – we actively care about others and participate in active service.

■ These Approaches to Learning (ATL) skills will be useful …

- Affective skills
- Collaboration skills
- Communication skills
- Creative-thinking skills
- Critical-thinking skills
- Information literacy skills
- Reflection skills
- Transfer skills

KEY WORDS

able-bodied	humour
deformity	point of view
disabled	syndrome
empathy	tension
genetic	

SENTENCE–PHRASE–WORD

1 Read the opening chapter, 'Ordinary', from *Wonder* by R.J. Palacio: https://bit.ly/38GM8oy and **identify**:
   - a sentence that is meaningful to you or captures the meaning of the chapter
   - a phrase that spoke to you in some way
   - a word that captured your attention or was powerful in some way.
2 **Justify** your choices, through discussion with a partner, and consider why these parts of the text stood out.
3 Now watch the trailer for the film version of *Wonder*: https://youtu.be/k3si7Vq8r7g.
4 In pairs, discuss the trailer and identify the themes that are explored and what you expect to happen in the book and film.

What is contemporary realistic fiction?

WHAT ARE THE CONVENTIONS OF THE REALISTIC GENRE?

Do you find the characters in the books that you read convincing? Do they seem real? Could they live in the 'real' world? **Contemporary realism** or **realistic fiction** tries to create characters that you could imagine living in the real world.

This genre is about people and events that are not real, but could be. The stories take place in a particular space and time, which we can identify by the characters and where the events occur. But what makes the stories realistic is the fact that they could happen in real life. It's important to remember, however, that this does not mean the stories are true.

The experiences of the author, either personal or researched, illustrate a life other than our own. When we see that life from the point of view of the imagined people living it, we gain a greater understanding of **audience imperatives**. In other words, we as readers engage and respond to the **context** and the themes of the story and, in doing so, make connections with our personal experience.

Through an analysis of the novel *Wonder* by R.J. Palacio, we will explore the impact that the relationships between the characters have on the development of identity.

Wonder by R.J. Palacio

This successful children's novel is written by R.J. Palacio and was published in 2012. It is a story about August 'Auggie' Pullman, a ten-year-old living with a rare medical facial deformity.

THINK–PAIR–SHARE

■ ATL

- Communication skills: Negotiate ideas and knowledge with peers and teachers

1 **Individually, make a list of your favourite TV shows or films.**
2 **Now in pairs, share your list. Discuss whether any of the television programmes or films have surreal elements, such as magic, or talking creatures. If they do, cross them off your list.**
3 **Identify how you connect with the remaining programmes or films on your list. Which characters do you relate to? What parts seem real or close to your life and experiences? How do you identify with these elements in the programmes and films?**

◆ Assessment opportunities

- ◆ In this activity you have practised skills that are assessed using Criterion D: Using language.

ACTIVITY: Realistic fiction

■ ATL

■ Communication skills: Use and interpret a range of discipline-specific terms and symbols

Watch this short introduction to realistic fiction: **https://bit.ly/3pTC0PG**.

1 In pairs or groups of three, **discuss** and share what you found out about realistic fiction from the video.
2 **Create** a list of the elements of realistic fiction. As you work through the activities in the chapter, add notes to your list.

◆ Assessment opportunities

◆ In this activity you have practised skills that are assessed using Criterion D: Using language.

Blurbs

A **blurb** is a short description of a book, film, etc which is used to sell and promote it. Take a look at these back cover blurbs for books.

What was once the western United States is now home to the Republic, a nation perpetually at war with its neighbors. Born into an elite family in one of the Republic's wealthiest districts, fifteen-year-old June is a prodigy being groomed for success in the Republic's highest military circles. Born into the slums, fifteen-year-old Day is the country's most wanted criminal. But his motives may not be as malicious as they seem.

From very different worlds, June and Day have no reason to cross paths – until the day June's brother, Metias, is murdered and Day becomes the prime suspect.

■ *Legend* by Marie Lu

'How about a story? Spin us a yarn.'

Instantly, Phoebe Winterbottom came to mind. 'I could tell you an extensively strange story,' I warned.

'Oh, good!' Gram said. 'Delicious!'

And that is how I happened to tell them about Phoebe, her disappearing mother, and the lunatic.

As Sal entertains her grandparents with Phoebe's outrageous story, her own story begins to unfold – the story of a thirteen-year-old girl whose only wish is to be reunited with her missing mother.

■ *Walk Two Moons* by Sharon Creech

Nine of us came here. We look like you. We talk like you. We live among you. But we are not you. We can do things you dream of doing. We have powers you dream of having. We are stronger and faster than anything you have ever seen. We are the superheroes you worship in movies and comic books – but we are real.

Our plan was to grow, and train, and become strong, and become one, and fight them. But they found us and started hunting us first. Now all of us are running. Spending our lives in shadows, in places where no one would look, blending in. We have lived among you without you knowing.

But *they* know.

They caught Number One in Malaysia.

Number Two in England.

And Number Three in Kenya.

They killed them all.

I am Number Four.

I am next.

■ *I Am Number Four* by Pittacus Lore

Ally has been smart enough to fool a lot of smart people. Every time she lands in a new school, she is able to hide her inability to read by creating clever yet disruptive distractions. She is afraid to ask for help; after all, how can you cure dumb? However, her newest teacher Mr Daniels sees the bright, creative kid underneath the trouble maker.

■ *Fish In A Tree* by Lynda Mullaly Hunt

A Year Without Mom follows 12-year-old Dasha through a year full of turmoil after her mother leaves for America. It is the early 1990s in Moscow, and political change is in the air. But Dasha is more worried about her own challenges as she negotiates family, friendships and school without her mother. Just as she begins to find her own feet, she gets word that she is to join her mother in America – a place that seems impossibly far from everything and everyone she loves.

■ *A Year Without Mom* by Dasha Tolstikova

Everyone says that middle school is awful, but Trent knows nothing could be worse than the year he had in fifth grade, when a freak accident on Cedar Lake left one kid dead, and Trent with a brain full of terrible thoughts he can't get rid of. Trent's pretty positive the entire disaster was his fault, so for him middle school feels like a fresh start, a chance to prove to everyone that he's not the horrible screw-up they seem to think he is.

If only Trent could make that fresh start *happen*.

■ *Lost in the Sun* by Lisa Graff

Phineas Gage was truly a man with a hole in his head. Phineas, a railroad construction foreman, was blasting rock near Cavendish, Vermont, in 1848 when a thirteen-pound iron rod was shot through his brain. Miraculously, he survived to live another eleven years and become a textbook case in brain science.

At the time, Phineas Gage seemed to completely recover from his accident. He could walk, talk, work, and travel, but he was changed. Gage 'was no longer Gage,' said his Vermont doctor, meaning that the old Phineas was dependable and well liked, and the new Phineas was crude and unpredictable.

His case astonished doctors in his day and still fascinates doctors today. What happened and what didn't happen inside the brain of Phineas Gage will tell you a lot about how your brain works and how you act human.

■ *Phineas Gage: A Gruesome but True Story About Brain Science* by John Fleischman

ACTIVITY: How do I know that I am reading a realistic fiction story?

■ ATL

■ Communication skills: Make inferences and draw conclusions

1 In pairs, **analyse** each back cover blurb (on pages 109–111) and **identify** the elements that make the storyline in the text realistic or at least possible. Select the blurbs that are realistic and those that seem unreal.
2 How can you make personal connections to the realistic elements in the texts? In pairs, **outline** the personal connections you made to each character, setting or plot.

◆ Assessment opportunities

◆ In this activity you have practised skills that are assessed using Criterion A: Analysing.

Where do authors find their inspiration?

Have you ever heard people say that they get their best ideas in the shower? Curiously, this seems to be true for many people, but it is not as strange as you might think. Researchers say that because of the monotony of taking a shower and the lack of mental stimulation – there isn't much to do besides stare at the wall or wash your hair – your brain goes on 'autopilot' and your unconscious mind is free to wander. As you daydream, your conscious mind is less likely to dismiss creative or unusual thoughts than when you are focusing very hard on a task, so more unconventional ideas float to the surface. This may be why some authors become inspired in places you wouldn't expect. They might suddenly have an idea while walking the dog, doing the dishes, or going grocery shopping.

However, there are many things around us that affect what thoughts and ideas we have in the first place, and therefore contribute to our inspiration. Many writers get inspiration from personal experiences, or the experiences of people close to them. Ernest Hemingway, for example, wrote *A Farewell to Arms*, in which the protagonist is an ambulance driver during the First World War, just as Hemingway himself had been. Authors also get inspiration from other writers and creative individuals. Often, literature and art movements form around a group of writers and artists who all have similar styles or ideas about society.

The key thing to remember about inspiration, though, is that it is not just an idea. Inspiration is the combination of emotion that comes from a powerful thought, and the passion that comes from a desire to explore this thought further.

ACTIVITY: Inspiration

ATL

- Communication skills: Write for different purposes; give and receive meaningful feedback
- Information literacy skills: Access information to be informed and inform others

Imagine you are an aspiring author who has been invited to interview R.J. Palacio about her book *Wonder,* and her profession as a writer. Among other things, you must find out how she got the inspiration to write *Wonder.*

1 First, make a list of questions you would like to ask her.
2 Now, carry out some online research about R.J. Palacio and her inspiration for writing *Wonder* and try to answer as many of your questions as you can. Create a collage with the information you have found about her.
3 Where did R.J. Palacio get her inspiration for *Wonder*?
4 Now, with your newfound information about R.J. Palacio, you are ready to write your own story. It does not have to be very long, but it should be about something that inspires you.

Did you know …

… you can contact R.J. Palacio to ask her questions about *Wonder*? Read the interview with R.J. Palacio at **https://n.pr/2LaozMf** and watch her speak at: **https://youtu.be/Hh5qbE62IyY**. Write a question that you have for the author that is not answered here. Try to contact the author and ask her your question via the **addresses** she provides on her website: **www.rjpalacio.com**.

Look through these helpful tips and prompt questions to help you find a topic and start writing:

- What activities do you enjoy? What holds your attention for long periods of time?
- Has anything very memorable or life-changing ever happened to you? How did it make you feel at the time? How does it make you feel now? Events that are very close and important to us are often the most inspirational.
- Try keeping a little notebook with you to jot down things you see or hear that you find interesting. You can use one of your notes as the inspiration for your story.
- Make lists of things you might want to write about.

5 Once you've chosen a topic, make a mind map of your ideas and then plot the outline of your story. Keep in mind that your story will need a plot, setting, characters and, importantly, a conflict of some kind. Make sure you include all of these elements.
6 Share your mind map with your partner and ask them to give you feedback.
7 Now, write your story.

◆ Assessment opportunities

- ◆ In this activity you have practised skills that are assessed using Criterion B: Organizing and Criterion D: Using language.

ACTIVITY: Writing a blurb

■ ATL

- ■ Communication skills: Read critically and for comprehension

At this point you will need your own copy of *Wonder*.

Task 1

1 In pairs, look at the first four chapters of *Wonder* and **identify** the realistic elements in the characters, settings and plot. Record them on sticky notes and don't forget to include the page references.
2 In the previous activity we looked at 'blurbs' found on the back cover of books. **Use** your notes and write your own 'blurb' for *Wonder*. Remember that the reader must be able to **identify** the story as 'realistic fiction'.
3 Share your blurb with your classmates.

Task 2

1 For each of the blurbs on pages 109–111, **select** descriptive words or phrases the author uses that are positive or negative. **Identify** language that is used to describe emotions.
2 In pairs, **discuss** the effect on the reader of using emotive language.

◆ Assessment opportunities

- ◆ In this activity you have practised skills that are assessed using Criterion C: Producing text and Criterion D: Using language.

ACTIVITY: Spelling bee

A spelling bee is a contest in which participants are asked to spell words of varying degrees of difficulty.

Task 1

In groups of four or five, make a list of words chosen from *Wonder* to use in a spelling bee. Be sure to include words of varying degrees of difficulty.

See the websites below for suggestions:
- https://bit.ly/3rg5N5G
- https://bit.ly/2Mudbvt
- https://bit.ly/36AfN1y

Now take part in a class spelling bee.

How to play

- Form equal-size teams of between three and ten players. You can line up or sit in circles. Decide on a set order in which the members of each team will play.
- The teacher will use the words that you have chosen from *Wonder*. They will choose a team to begin and call out a word for that team to spell; they can also use the word in a sentence to give the word context.
- Everyone on the first team takes turns calling out one letter of the word at a time; the first student on the team calls out the first letter of the word, the second person calls out the second letter, and so on. If the word has four or more letters and the team has only three members, then play returns to the first person on the team after the third letter is called out. If the team spells the word correctly, they earn one point and play moves to the second team. If the second team spells their word correctly, they earn one point and play moves to the third team.
- When a team spells a word incorrectly, play passes immediately to the next team. If that team spells the word correctly, they earn two points (the one they earned and the one that would have been given to the first team if they had spelled the word correctly). If the second team spells the word incorrectly, play passes to the third team, which earns three points if they spell the word correctly. At the end of the game, the team with the most points are the winners.

Task 2

Take the *Wonder* vocabulary quiz and see how many new words you have learnt. Click on the flashcards link to play the game: https://bit.ly/3reOdyN.

How to improve your spelling

- When you are practising spellings, use as many senses as you can:
  - look closely at a word and try to remember what it *looks* like
  - think about the *sound* of a word, as this will often give you clues about the spelling
  - to learn a word, *write* it or *type* it – or both.
- Never use capitals when writing down words to learn – the shape of a word written in lower case letters helps your visual memory.
- To make your learning personal to you, start a Spelling Record – your own personal dictionary.
- Dictionaries are helpful. Remember you can also use an online dictionary or thesaurus.
- Reading will help you improve your spelling. Don't just read books, but everything around you, such as newspapers, catalogues, adverts and posters.
- If you are not sure how to spell a word, try out different spellings. Often you will be able to tell which one looks right. For example, *rythm, rhythym – rhythm.*
- Always proofread your work. Why not ask a friend or a family member to read your work too?

EXTENSION

English spelling may be a nightmare but there are ways to help you become a better speller.

Do you know what a 'blunder' is? A **synonym** for blunder is error.

Visit this website and find some other synonyms for blunder: **www.synonymy.com**.

Keeping a Blunder Book can help you become a better writer. The idea is a simple one: keep a record of words you spell incorrectly (using the correct spelling, of course) or create a document on the computer. Look through your list before you proofread your work. Keep your list updated by removing words you know how to spell and adding new ones.

Learn about other strategies that can help you improve your spelling: **https://bit.ly/3tdtBc2**.

Did you know …

… that spelling bees began in 1925, when the first competition was organized by *The Courier-Journal* in Kentucky, USA? They have been popular ever since. Some spelling bees can last for two days!

■ Fainali, xen, aafte sam 20 iers ov orxogrefkl riform, wi wud hev a lojikl, kohirnt speling in ius xrewawt xe Ingliy-spiking werld. – M.J.Shields
https://bit.ly/2O0o2Ob

Carry out some research and find out about **fundraising ideas through organizing a spelling bee**. Why not organize one in your school to support one of your school's nominated charities?

Does realistic fiction portray all of the aspects of the real world?

Many of the stories in realistic fiction explore the joy, pain and humour we experience in life. In fact, the wide range of ideas, opinions and questions that make up human existence may be more obvious in realistic fiction than in our own lives. Good stories do not resolve serious conflict with easy answers, but may allow us to see the issue in a different light. Realistic fiction weaves universal values, like honesty, loyalty, responsibility and resilience, into a story that often requires characters to overcome difficulties in their lives by relying on their inner strength or resolving a personal problem.

ACTIVITY: Discovering the self

ATL

- Affective skills: Resilience – Practice 'bouncing back' after adversity, mistakes and failures
- Communication skills: Organize and depict information logically

In *Wonder,* characters engage in a journey of self-discovery.

1 In pairs, focus on two of the characters and **list** the things they discover about themselves and how they do so. What challenges do they face? What steps do the characters take to overcome the challenges you have identified?
2 Think about your own experiences. How do they compare or differ?
3 In pairs, think about the steps you can take to overcome some of the challenges you have noted.
4 Now **create** a character of your own. Copy and complete the table below.

Character	
Situation	
Character's problem/ predicament	
Resolution	

5 Use the prompts below to help you make notes about your chosen character.
  - What does the character look like?
  - What does the character do?
  - What does the character say?
  - How do they relate to other characters?
  - What do other characters say about them?
  - What are the strengths of the character? What are the weaknesses?
  - What motivates the character? **Justify** your answer by referring to a particular incident in the story.
  - How does the character feel?
  - Does the character face any challenges? How does the character try to overcome the challenges?
6 **Organize** your notes and ideas to write a descriptive paragraph. Be creative and use words and images in your paragraph.

◆ Assessment opportunities

- ◆ In this activity you have practised skills that are assessed using Criterion A: Analysing, Criterion B: Organizing and Criterion C: Producing text.

■ American singer-songwriter and musician, Natalie Merchant

WHO IS THE NARRATOR?

Who is the narrator? What is their role in the story? *Wonder* is narrated in the first person throughout, although this doesn't mean that it's the *same* person speaking directly to us.

In Chapter 2 (page 53) we examined narrative voice and saw that authors use different narrative techniques to offer various perspectives on the action of the story. In *Wonder*, R.J. Palacio uses first person narration to provide an intimate account of August's experience of growing up and living with a genetic deformity.

The first person voice allows the reader to put themselves in the narrator's shoes and clearly see their perspective. This creates a sense of empathy for the narrator and an immediacy to the story. In *Wonder*, we are offered the viewpoint of those closest to August, and gain an insight into their feelings and experiences as they relate to him. Everyone has a story.

However, there is only one person describing the stories of many. What challenges does an author face in choosing to write a novel in multiple voices?

ACTIVITY: 'Wonder' by Natalie Merchant

■ ATL

- ■ Information literacy skills: Make connections between various sources of information
- ■ Collaboration skills: Practise empathy

As you will have discovered, Palacio was inspired by Natalie Merchant's song, 'Wonder'. Listen to or read the lyrics to her song:
https://youtu.be/6zpYFAzhAZY
and **https://bit.ly/3assj4h**.

As you listen or read, make connections with the novel. **Compare and contrast** how Merchant's attitude to being a 'wonder' and the reactions of others around her are similar to or different from August's attitude and the reactions of others around him.

EXTENSION

Carry out some research about Treacher Collins syndrome and write down five facts about the syndrome.

As you research, consider the following questions:
- In what ways are people with physical disabilities perceived differently from able-bodied people?
- Do disabled people face prejudice or discrimination that able-bodied people do not experience? Why do you think this is or is not the case?

Give a three-minute presentation to your classmates, sharing the information you have found.

◆ Assessment opportunities

- ◆ In this activity you have practised skills that are assessed using Criterion D: Using language.

ACTIVITY: Narrative point of view

Task 1

1 In pairs, **identify** the narrative voice in *Wonder*. How do the different narrative voices offer new points of view?
2 Auggie's face is not completely described until later in the story, in Via's chapter 'August: Through the Peephole'. **Evaluate** why the author has chosen to leave the description of Auggie until then.
   - What effect did this choice have on your opinion of Auggie and his experience?
   - How close is this description to your own mental picture of Auggie?
   - Did you have a picture of his face in your mind while reading the book? Did this description change that picture?

Task 2

1 **Examine** the impact adults have on Auggie. How do Auggie's parents, teachers and other adults affect his life?
2 Look at the emails between Mr Tushman, Julian's parents, and Jack's parents in the chapter 'Letters, Emails, Facebook, Texts'. Up to this point in the story we have only seen how the children at Auggie's school have reacted to him.
   - Is Mrs Albans' attitude towards Auggie different from that of the other adults?
   - What do you make of her statement that Auggie is 'handicapped'?
   - Do you think she is correct in her belief that asking 'ordinary' children, like Julian, to befriend Auggie is unfair?

Task 3

Wonder is August's story. However, in the novel, six different characters tell their versions of the story in the first person.

1 In pairs, look back at the different parts and **identify** whose point of view is highlighted in each section. What impact do the varying points of view have on the reader?
2 Now, let's focus on Via, Auggie's sister.
   Discuss Via's point of view. How does point of view influence a character's description of an event? What are the author's intentions? Consider the challenges an author faces to make different voices sound real and convincing.
3 In the opening part of Via's chapter there is a quote taken from the lyrics of David Bowie's song, 'Space Oddity': 'Planet Earth is blue and there's nothing I can do.' This is the song that Miranda and Auggie used to love to sing together when Auggie was little.
   Listen to the complete song: https://youtu.be/iYYRH4apXDo.
   As you listen, answer the following questions:
   - What is the song about?
   - What **point of view** is expressed?
   - What mood is created?
   - How does the song affect Via?
   - How does it relate to Auggie?
4 In pairs, write a two-person narrative in which a story is told from one point of view, then another. Each voice might be heard one or multiple times.
5 Collate and compile your narratives into a class book of short stories.

ACTIVITY: Tug of war

Look at the chapters 'First-Day Jitters', 'Locks' and 'Around the Room'. These chapters highlight August's first experiences at school. The issue of August's possible attendance at a real school creates conflict for the characters in the novel, as they must decide what they think is best, and may find that they disagree with others.

In groups of three, consider the following dilemma: Should August attend Beecher School or continue to be home-schooled?

- **Identify** the factors that 'pull' at each side of the dilemma. These are the two sides of the tug of war.
- **Now think of why you support one side of the dilemma. Try to think of reasons on the other side of the dilemma as well.**
- Generate 'What if?' questions to **explore** the topic further. For example: *What if August is bullied at school because of his appearance?*

▼ Links to: Individuals and societies

Through these subjects we can explore all kinds of cultures in terms of race, gender, age, class, family structure, religion, abilities and regions.

Use the diversity of your school community to appreciate and celebrate difference. Look for common – but possibly unlikely – bonds which will help you to see yourself in the person who is most unlike you.

Humorous techniques

Here are some humorous techniques used by writers:

- The **'double *as*'** technique, where the word 'as' is used twice in a sentence. For example: *He was as dumb as Lois Lane, not figuring out Clark Kent is Superman!*
- The **'so'** technique. For example: *It was so cold out, the polar bear's teeth were chattering!*
- A serious-sounding sentence made humorous by adding a **comment in brackets**. For example:

My brother, who was always in trouble in school, is now in the legal system (doing time).

- The most popular technique is **exaggeration**. For example: *He has a brain the size of a pea.*
- Then there is the opposite of exaggeration, which is the **'understatement'** or **'shrinking'** technique. For example: *The man who painted our house charged by the hour and used a watercolour paintbrush.*

ACTIVITY: What's in a 'precept'?

■ ATL

- Creative-thinking skills: Create original works and ideas; use existing works and ideas in new ways

1 **Examine** the chapter 'Choose Kind' *from Wonder*.
2 In pairs, **consider** the precepts in speech bubbles below. What does each one mean?

> You must do the thing you think you cannot do.

■ Eleanor Roosevelt

> The bamboo that bends is stronger than the oak that resists.

■ Japanese proverb

> And above all, watch with glittering eyes the whole world around you because the greatest secrets are always hidden in the most unlikely places. Those who don't believe in magic will never find it.

■ Roald Dahl, *The Minpins*

3 What does the word 'precept' mean? Write your own definition for the word. Use a dictionary of your choice and check your definition. Were you right?
4 Do we all have precepts that we live by? Where do you think precepts come from?
5 Mr Browne's precepts play an important part in *Wonder*. Mr Browne has his students send him their own precept over the summer holiday.

    In pairs or groups of three, **create** your own precept with an explanation. You can also look for inspiration in a song lyric, quotation from a novel, a famous saying or something personal between your friends and family.

ACTIVITY: What can you infer?

■ ATL

- Communication skills: Use appropriate forms of writing for different purposes and audiences; use and interpret a range of discipline-specific terms and symbols

Narrative tension is the suspense that keeps the reader reading and wondering what will happen next. In *Wonder*, Palacio uses tension and humour to develop the plot and present events that may be difficult or sad. Auggie and his family have lots of jokes together, and both Auggie and Jack have a great sense of humour.

1 Refer to the 'Humorous techniques' box on page 119, and see how many you can **identify** in *Wonder*.

    Analyse the role humour plays in helping the family cope with their situation.
2 In pairs, **discuss** this quote by George Orwell:

    'Whatever is funny is subversive.'

    What do you think this quote means?

3 In pairs or groups of three, go to Google images and select six to ten photographs. **Create** captions for your photographs and apply a variety of humorous strategies.
4 Have a go at some humorous writing, following these guidelines:
- Try to make your reader laugh with you. Try making fun of yourself.
- Try to be specific and give details rather than use generalizations.
- Use funny words, phrases and sentences. Think carefully about the vocabulary you use. Use an online thesaurus and dictionary.
- Make sure you edit your text and get feedback from a classmate.

◆ Assessment opportunities

◆ In this activity you have practised skills that are assessed using Criterion A: Analysing, Criterion C: Producing text and Criterion D: Using language.

7 In the chapter 'Mr Browne's October Precept', a precept from Mr Browne is: 'Your deeds are your monuments.'
   - What do you think this means? Do you agree? Why? Why not?
   - In your own words, explain whether you agree or disagree with the idea in this precept.
8 How might the message of the precepts and quotes you have read and created apply to our lives in class, in school, at home and in our community?
9 **Create** a display in your classroom and write your precepts on sticky notes. Take turns in choosing a precept and make it the motto or class rule for that week.
10 In this same chapter, Auggie writes a piece on being remembered for the things we do. Write a paragraph **analysing** Auggie's response.

◆ Assessment opportunities

- In this activity you have practised skills that are assessed using Criterion C: Producing text and Criterion D: Using language.

ⓘ Different types of verbal and written humour

banter friendly mutual teasing; exchange of witty remarks

blunder joke based on a person who makes a mistake, which makes them appear silly

caricature exaggeration of a person's mental, physical, or personality characteristic

conundrum a challenging word puzzle that can be difficult to solve, for example, *What goes up and never goes down? Your age.*

exaggeration an exaggerated remark that emphasizes the traits, defects or uniqueness of someone or something

Freudian slip a funny statement made accidentally, that is, without thinking, but which actually comes from the person's subconscious thoughts

hyperbole extreme exaggeration

! Take Action

! Why not create a monthly precepts podcast at your school?

   ◆ Each month, ask students from a different class to come up with some precepts from which you (along with a team of other students) choose one to feature in the podcast.

   ◆ You may need to ask a teacher to help you record your podcasts.

irony using words to express something completely different from the literal meaning (usually, someone says the opposite of what they mean and the listener believes the opposite of what they said)

joke short story with a funny or unexpected ending

parody humorous interpretation of any famous writing

practical joke a joke put into action (the trick is played on another person and the humour comes from what happens)

recovery a combination of blunder and wit, where a person makes a mistake, and then saves the situation by making a quick correction

repartee conversation that includes clever responses (the most common form is the insult)

satire wit that is critical humour; sarcasm that makes fun of something

situational humour comedy that is based on a funny situation

understatement making something of a normal size seem smaller or unimportant; intentionally downplaying an object or situation

wisecrack a quick and clever remark about a particular person or thing

wit humour, irony, sarcasm, satire, repartee (wit is amusing because of the sudden delivery of the remark which can be hurtful towards a person)

wordplay playful or clever use of words

I definitely experienced forms of bullying, and that's why it's so important for me to write songs like 'Beautiful' and 'Fighter'.

■ Pop singer, Christina Aguilera

■ 'Beautiful Child' is a song from the album *Peace*, the final studio album by the British band Eurythmics, released in October 1999

ACTIVITY: Beauty is in the eye of the beholder

■ ATL

- Collaboration skills: Practise empathy
- Affective skills: Self-motivation – practise positive thinking
- Reflection skills: Focus on the process of creating by imitating the work of others

1 Throughout the book *Wonder* there are many references to songs. Auggie and Nate have fun reciting the lines from a favourite song 'The Luckiest Guy on the Lower East Side', which was written by Stephen Merritt and performed by The Magnetic Fields. What does this song mean to them?

2 Listen to or read the lyrics (www.azlyrics.com/lyrics) to the following songs that are mentioned in *Wonder*. As you listen make notes on what the songs say or imply about beauty.
- 'Beautiful' by Christina Aguilera: https://youtu.be/eAfyFTzZDMM
- 'Beautiful Things' by Andain: https://youtu.be/DZePcUR097Q
- 'Beautiful Child' by Eurythmics: https://youtu.be/azBjWMz3yek

3 In pairs, **consider** what beauty is.
- What do you do to feel attractive?
- How would it feel if you had a facial disfigurement that you couldn't hide?

4 **Interpret** the meaning of each song. Which song means the most to you? **Justify** your answer with quotes from the song.

5 **Identify** any other literary devices, for example, personification, simile or metaphor used in the songs.

6 Why do you think the author refers to these songs in the novel?

7 Now, write your own song. **Analyse** the lyrics and focus on the language features of your favourite song. Write a song about your class and the things you do in it. Start by brainstorming as many different things about your class as you can think of and what makes your class special.

◆ Assessment opportunities

◆ In this activity you have practised skills that are assessed using Criterion A: Analysing, Criterion C: Producing text and Criterion D: Using language.

EXTENSION

Carry out some research about a Victorian man named Joseph Merrick, more famously known as the Elephant Man.

Write a paragraph **explaining** how his situation could relate to that of Auggie.

▼ Links to: Physical and health education

In your lessons, suggest films and activities that introduce discussion about why bullies target and tease others due to their differences. Take a stand against bullying by promoting cultural diversity in your school and encouraging your peers to speak out against unacceptable behaviour.

ACTIVITY: Asking the right questions

■ ATL

■ Transfer skills: Apply skills and knowledge in unfamiliar situations

You may have noticed that this chapter is different from the others in the book. There are no inquiry questions at the beginning.

1 In pairs, look at the beginning of the chapters in this book and focus on the three types of inquiry questions.
   - What three categories are used to organize the questions?
   - What is the purpose of these questions?
   - Which types of questions do you use most frequently?
   - What makes a good question?
   - Which questions do you find motivating and exciting?
2 Now, in groups of three, write factual, conceptual and debatable questions for this chapter. The question matrix available at https://bit.ly/3nInPhQ could assist you in this task.
3 As a class, select the best questions for each category for this chapter. Consider the tasks in the chapter when you make your selection.

◆ Assessment opportunities

◆ In this activity you have practised skills that are assessed using Criterion C: Producing text and Criterion D: Using language.

ACTIVITY: Bullying

■ ATL

■ Affective skills: Emotional management – Practise strategies to prevent and eliminate bullying

1 Carry out some research on the subject of bullying. Is it on the rise? What forms can it take? What role does social media play in bullying? Where does it most often occur and how do people react to or stop it? Use online resources and library books, and consider interviewing your school counsellor or another adult to help you with your research.
2 Use the findings from your research to write a persuasive essay on the best way to stop and prevent bullying. Remember to support and **justify** your argument with documented evidence.
   Remember, emotional messages and personal or anecdotal experiences can be persuasive, but must be balanced by verifiable fact. Make sure you use a variety of **primary** and **secondary sources** to give your research credibility.
3 **Discuss** the topic of bullying further as a class. Is it possible to take a strong personal stand against bullying?

◆ Assessment opportunities

◆ In this activity you have practised skills that are assessed using Criterion B: Organizing, Criterion C: Producing text and Criterion D: Using language.

'Be kind, for everyone you meet is fighting a harder battle.' – Plato

! Through a focused reading of the novel *Wonder* by R.J. Palacio, we have been able to look beyond the text and **evaluate** how drama, discussion and creative expression can encourage us to express feelings of empathy. We have focused on how kindness and acceptance of who we are as individuals encourages personal growth.

! Think of ways you can work with your school community or student council to help students to recognize their own fears and personal doubts.

! Take part in R.J. Palacio's initiative and take the Certified Kind Challenge. Find out more here: **http://choosekind.tumblr.com/certified-kind-classroom-challenge**.

Reflection

In this chapter, we have learnt how contemporary realistic fiction allows us to make **connections** and view the complex **relationships** that exist within families, friendship groups and at school from a different perspective. Even if our personal experiences and **contexts** are different from what we read about, these stories allow us to feel empathy and use their conclusions in our own lives. Furthermore, we have discovered that in realistic fiction, the author includes their own **point of view** and moral beliefs in their portrayal of characters and events. It is not a distant and unbiased representation of a situation that we are reading about, but a way for the author to express their values to a wide **audience**.

Use this table to reflect on your own learning in this chapter.						
Questions we asked		Answers we found	Any further questions now?			
Factual:						
Conceptual:						
Debatable:						
Approaches to learning you used in this chapter:		Description – what new skills did you learn?	How well did you master the skills?			
			Novice	Learner	Practitioner	Expert
Affective skills						
Collaboration skills						
Communication skills						
Creative-thinking skills						
Critical-thinking skills						
Information literacy skills						
Reflection skills						
Transfer skills						
Learner profile attribute(s)		*Reflect on the importance of being caring for your learning in this chapter.*				
Caring						

SOME SUMMATIVE TASKS TO TRY

Use these tasks to apply and extend your learning in this chapter. These tasks are designed so that you can evaluate your learning at different levels of achievement in the Language and literature criteria.

THIS TASK CAN BE USED TO EVALUATE YOUR LEARNING IN CRITERION B AND CRITERION D

Task 1: Radio play

For this task, you will select a scene from *Wonder* and convert it into a radio play.

What is a radio play? To find out, listen to the beginning of *The War of the Worlds* written by H.G. Wells and recorded by Orson Welles in 1938: **https://youtu.be/OzC3Fg_rRJM**.

As you listen, answer the questions below:
- What do you think this is about?
- How has the author created meaning?

You have just experienced a radio play. It's a form of audio storytelling broadcast on radio, with no visual elements. A radio play relies on dialogue, music and sound effects to help the listener imagine the story.

To **create** your own radio play you will need to write a script.

Explore **examples of scripts** here:
- **www.bbc.co.uk/writersroom/scripts**
- **https://bbc.in/3j9WD7I**
- **www.simplyscripts.com**

Now, it's your turn. In groups of three or five, choose a scene from *Wonder* and start to plan a radio performance based on your chosen part of the novel. Consider the following:
- Characters with dialogue
- Sound effects (For ideas on how to create sound effects for your radio play visit: **www.epicsound.com/sfx**.)
- Speeches and monologues
- The role of the narrator
- How to grab the attention of the audience and keep them interested.

Before you can start recording you must think about how you will deliver your lines and practise your finished script.

The radio play should be about three to five minutes long.

Task 2: Auggie's parents

In this chapter you have considered the narrative point of view in *Wonder*. You might have been surprised to find that we do not hear from Auggie's parents. Why do you think the author has not given them a voice?

Rewrite a scene in the novel from the point of view of Auggie's parents.

Task 3: How can one person affect others?

August Pullman's appearance has affected everyone in his life and the way people react to his appearance has affected him.

Choose one character from the story and **describe** how his or her actions, words or attitude have affected others. Use specific examples from the story in your response.

6 Is all the world a stage?

Through the **genre** of drama, Shakespeare has made **connections** with **audiences** across the globe for centuries, demonstrating the power of literature to transcend **space and time**.

CONSIDER THESE QUESTIONS:

Factual: Who was William Shakespeare? Was Shakespeare a poet or a playwright? What is a sonnet? What is a play?

Conceptual: How can Shakespeare's plays teach us about people and society? How are women presented in Shakespeare's plays? Why are there so many speeches in Shakespeare's plays?

Debatable: Are the themes explored in Shakespeare's plays as relevant today as when they were written? Is something lost in translation when we perform Shakespeare in other languages?

Now **share and compare** your thoughts and ideas with your partner, or with the whole class.

IN THIS CHAPTER, WE WILL ...

- **Find out** about who Shakespeare was and what he wrote.
- **Explore** the impact of Shakespeare's work on literature, art and film across the globe.
- **Take action** to find engaging ways in which you can bring Shakespeare to people of your age group and to overcome the obstacles we face when we're trying to understand concepts and language that we may find difficult.

■ These Approaches to Learning (ATL) skills will be useful …

- Collaboration skills
- Communication skills
- Creative-thinking skills
- Critical-thinking skills
- Information literacy skills
- Media literacy skills

● We will reflect on this learner profile attribute …

- Inquirers – we nurture our curiosity, developing skills for inquiry and research.

◆ Assessment opportunities in this chapter:

- **Criterion A:** Analysing
- **Criterion B:** Organizing
- **Criterion C:** Producing text
- **Criterion D:** Using language

DISCUSS

Are you a Shakespeare buff? Let's find out …

Answer the questions below individually and see how much you know about Shakespeare. In pairs, **compare** your answers and complete any gaps you may have.

1 When was Shakespeare born?
2 Where was he born?
3 Do we know where Shakespeare went to school?
4 What were his parents' names?
5 In 1582 Shakespeare was married, but to whom?
6 Shakespeare had three children. What were their names?
7 Shakespeare died on his birthday in what year?
8 How many plays did Shakespeare write?
9 How many sonnets is he believed to have written?
10 Approximately how many new words is Shakespeare supposed to have created?
   a 150   b 1,000
   c 3,000   d 10,000

KEY WORDS

adaptation	play	theatre
drama	stage	

Who was William Shakespeare?

Shakespeare this, Shakespeare that … It seems the whole world is talking about William Shakespeare. So, what's all the fuss about? Who is this man and why can't we seem to get enough of him?

William Shakespeare was a poet and playwright who lived in England during the 16th and 17th centuries. He is considered to be one of the most important writers of all time and his 38 plays have been translated into many different languages.

Shakespeare's work has had a profound impact on our literary and cultural heritage. His writing has helped shape the English language we use today and his plays are considered essential reading in classrooms across the globe.

Plays, according to one of his most famous characters, Hamlet, 'hold as 'twere the mirror up to nature' and Shakespeare's plays do precisely that. The universal themes explored in his writing mean something to audiences today, just as they did to the people of his time; his richly woven plots and three-dimensional characters allow us to gain a deeper insight into human nature. Perhaps this is where the secret to Shakespeare's enduring appeal lies.

In this chapter we will delve into the life, times and literature of William Shakespeare and find out why his work is as relevant today as it was when it was first written.

William Shakespeare: A life in five 'facts'

While we know a lot about Shakespeare's works, we know less about his personal life.

Date of birth: We don't actually know. We *do* know that he was baptised on 26 April 1564. As the tradition was to baptise children three days after their birth, we can assume that he was born on 23 April, which is the date we use today to celebrate his birthday.

Place of birth: Now this we know! Shakespeare was born in a small town called Stratford-upon-Avon, which is now a popular tourist attraction.

Education: This may surprise you, but Shakespeare probably didn't stay in school for as long as most of you will have to. He is believed to have started school at the age of seven, and probably finished his schooling at the age of fifteen. School started at six o'clock in the morning and finished at six o'clock in the evening. He learnt Latin mostly, and girls were not allowed to go to school.

Career: Shakespeare's life in the theatre actually began as an actor. There is much speculation about what Shakespeare did before he joined an acting troupe that would lead him to London where he would eventually become a playwright.

Shakespeare was also a bit of businessman and he became quite wealthy by the end of the sixteenth century.

Death: On 23 April 1616, Shakespeare died in his hometown at New Place, the second biggest house in town. In 1759 the owner of the house, the local vicar, had it pulled down as he was fed up with the constant stream of visitors.

GOOD FREND FOR IESVS SAKE FORBEARE,
TO DIGG THE DVST ENCLOASED HEARE:
BLESE BE Y MAN Y SPARES HES STONES,
AND CVRST BE HE Y MOVES MY BONES.

■ Literary to the end: Shakespeare's sinister warning inscribed on his gravestone to deter people from stealing his remains. But did it work? Sadly no, as archaeologists confirmed in 2016, that Shakespeare's skull is missing.

Did you know …

… that a bard was a 'professional' storyteller in medieval times? Because of the major contribution Shakespeare made to English literature, many feel that he is deserving of this title, and that's why you'll often hear him referred to as 'the Bard'.

Exploring context

When we study literature, it is absolutely essential that we have an awareness of context. But what exactly does this mean? Well, the context of a text is the place and time in which it was written, who it was written by and where it was published. All of these have an impact on the purpose and effect of the text.

When we consider context we ask certain questions, such as:

- What was society like at the time the text was written?
- What or who influenced the writer?
- What important social or political events are reflected in the text?
- Does the text conform to the conventions of the genre? How does it fit in with other works of literature written at the time?
- Is the text set in the period when it was written? If not, why not? And if so, what can we learn from this?

Not only does exploring context enhance our appreciation of a work of literature, but it helps us to develop a deeper understanding of the author and their purpose for writing. By looking into social and historical context, we can learn about the hopes and anxieties of people across time and space.

▼ Links to: Individuals and societies: History

Shakespeare's world

Have you studied the sixteenth and seventeenth centuries in your Individuals and societies lessons? What do you imagine life was like in England in those days? What do you know about people's attitudes and beliefs at the time?

In pairs or groups of three, carry out some research about Shakespeare's world. Choose one of the following categories and prepare a one-page handout, in your own words, for your peers. Ask your teacher to collate your handouts into a *Shakespeare's World: Context* handbook.

- Royalty and the state
- Exploration and conquest
- Shakespeare's London
- Religion
- Knowledge – science and the arts

In this chapter, we will consider how some of these contexts are reflected in Shakespeare's writing, and learn about the anxieties which played on the minds of people during the sixteenth and seventeenth centuries.

Did you know …

… that there were no dictionaries until 1604? This means that language used in this era was very fluid and could be moulded and shaped.

… that Shakespeare introduced lots of new words to the English language? Watch this short clip and see how many you can spot: **https://youtu.be/BMkuUADWW2A**.

Was Shakespeare a poet or a playwright?

WHAT IS A PLAY?

Today, when we hear Shakespeare's name, many of us think of his plays – *Romeo and Juliet* and *Hamlet* are just two of many which spring to mind. But we mustn't forget that he was also a poet, and a pretty good one too.

However, Shakespeare is mostly associated with drama so it's important that we give his plays the attention they deserve. By the time Shakespeare picked up a quill to write his first play in the late sixteenth century, drama as a literary form had been around for at least two thousand years.

So, what exactly are plays and why do we still flock to theatres today to watch them? A play is a literary text, written by a **playwright**, in which a story unfolds through action and **dialogue** between characters. The word 'wright' means 'maker', so a playwright is literally a maker of plays. Plays are written to be performed, usually live on stage, by actors at a theatre, and the events that make up the plot are organized and divided using **acts** and **scenes**. The characters in a play are crucially important as it is their dialogue, actions and relationships that drive the plot forward.

Sounds a bit like a film? Well, yes and no. Lots of plays are adapted for the big screen and film scripts are a bit like playscripts. The crucial difference, however, is that on stage there is absolutely no room for error. On a film set, where a single scene can be shot several times over, you may be forgiven for forgetting your lines now and then; however, on stage, in front of a living, breathing audience, an actor has no choice but to get it right first time.

Making sense of Shakespeare: Iambic pentameter

When you begin to read Shakespeare's writing out loud, you can't miss the fact there is often a rhythm to his words. In fact, a large proportion of his plays are written in verse. He was, after all, a poet at heart.

Shakespeare alternates between **prose** and poetry in his plays for a number of reasons. One reason is to help us, as the audience, to identify the social class of the characters in a play. Characters of a higher social status, such as royals or members of the nobility, are often allocated lines written in verse, whereas those lower in the social hierarchy, such as people of the working classes or peasants, say their lines in prose.

When Shakespeare did write in verse, his preferred rhythm was **iambic pentameter**. But what exactly is this?

Watch the short video to find out what iambic pentameter is and to develop an understanding of why it is used: **https://youtu.be/I5lsuyUNu_4**.

As you watch, answer the following questions:
- **Identify** three effects of iambic pentameter and write them down.
- According to the video, what are two easy ways to help you remember what iambic pentameter is?

Now let's see if we can **identify** the rhythm ourselves.

Read 'Sonnet 18' on page 131, and highlight the stressed beats. Remember, there are ten beats to a line in iambic pentameter.

Have some fun performing the poem to other members of your group. After all, poetry was written to be recited.

There is something quite magical about seeing a play come together on stage. Each performance is unique, different from other performances due to subtle improvisations; the atmosphere is altered by the mood and energy of the audience, a different one each night. And this magic and wonder is only enhanced by the staging of the works of William Shakespeare.

WHAT IS A SONNET?

Although well known for his plays, Shakespeare was ultimately a poet and wrote an incredible 154 sonnets during his lifetime.

A **sonnet** is a fourteen-line poem, which has a very specific **rhythm** and **rhyme**. The form, which originated in Italy, is commonly used for love poems. Shakespeare adapted the structure slightly and thus the Shakespearean (or as it is also known, the Elizabethan) sonnet was born.

Here's one for us to explore.

ACTIVITY: What is a sonnet?

■ ATL

■ Communication skills: Read critically and for comprehension

Read 'Sonnet 18' and then answer the following questions:

1 What suggests that this is a poem about love?
2 Explain the effect of the use of **direct address** in the poem?
3 Find an example of **personification** in the poem and comment on the effect.
4 At which point do you think the mood of the poem changes?
5 What does the narrator identify as the major difference between 'a summer's day' and the person to whom the poem is addressed?

◆ Assessment opportunities

◆ In this activity you have practised skills that are assessed using Criteria A: Analysing.

A sonnet usually begins with three **quatrains** (four-line stanzas).

Shakespearean sonnets are written in **iambic pentameter**.

Sonnet 18

Shall I compare thee to a summer's day?
Thou art more lovely and more temperate.
Rough winds do shake the darling buds of May,
And summer's lease hath all too short a date.
Sometime too hot the eye of heaven shines,
And often is his gold complexion dimmed;
And every fair from fair sometime declines,
By chance, or nature's changing course, untrimmed;
But thy eternal summer shall not fade,
Nor lose possession of that fair thou ow'st,
Nor shall death brag thou wand'rest in his shade,
When in eternal lines to time thou grow'st.
So long as men can breathe, or eyes can see,
So long lives this, and this gives life to thee.

There is often an **alternate rhyme** scheme which varies in each quatrain (abab cdcd efef).

Shakespearean sonnets end with a **couplet** (gg). A couplet is a pair of successive lines (lines that follow one another) of **verse**, typically rhyming and of the same length.

The **volta** usually still comes with the ninth line, but in *some* of Shakespeare's sonnets it comes with the thirteenth. In a sonnet, a volta is the point at which the argument, idea or mood of the poem changes.

ACTIVITY: Tragedy, comedy, history or problem play?

■ ATL

- Communication skills: Organize and depict information logically
- Collaboration skills: Listen actively to other perspectives and ideas

1 Shakespeare wrote over 30 plays and they mainly fall into these categories. Match the category with its definition:

Category	Definition
Comedy	Shakespeare based these plays on real events that he had read about. He sometimes altered events slightly.
History	At the end of the play almost everyone dies. At least one of the characters has a **tragic flaw**.
Tragedy	At the end of the play all the characters live happily ever after, but they have had to overcome many obstacles.

2 Some of the plays cannot be classified so easily and are referred to as 'problem plays'.

   Take a look at these Shakespeare titles and categorize them:
   - Tragedy
   - Comedy
   - History
   - Problem play

A Midsummer Night's Dream
All's Well That Ends Well
Antony and Cleopatra
As You Like It
Comedy of Errors
Coriolanus
Cymbeline
Hamlet
Henry IV, part i
Henry IV, part ii
Henry V
Henry VI, part i
Henry VI, part ii
Henry VI, part iii
Henry VIII
Julius Caesar
King John
King Lear
Macbeth
Measure for Measure
Merchant of Venice
Merry Wives of Windsor
Much Ado About Nothing
Othello
Pericles
Richard II
Richard III
Romeo and Juliet
The Taming of the Shrew
The Tempest
The Winter's Tale
Timon of Athens
Titus Andronicus
Troilus and Cressida
Twelfth Night
Two Gentlemen of Verona

3 Share your answers with a partner. Make sure you **justify** your choices. How many did you get right?

◆ Assessment opportunities

◆ In this activity you have practised skills that are assessed using Criterion B: Organizing.

▼ Links to: Drama

Although the starting point of any theatre production is the play itself, the success of a dramatic performance depends on a number of elements. Match the following terms to their definitions.

Aside	Part of the script of a play that tells the actors how they are to move or to speak their lines (usually written in brackets).
Stage directions	The arrangement of scenery, used to identify the setting of the play.
Props	When a character's dialogue is spoken but not heard by the other actors on the stage.
Stage set	The garments worn by actors, used to indicate the characters they are playing.
Costumes	Objects used on stage by actors during a performance.

'[Exit, pursued by a bear]' from *The Winter's Tale* is quite possibly one of the most memorable stage directions in drama.

The most famous theatre for the staging of Shakespeare's plays is the Globe, which overlooks the River Thames in London: **https://bit.ly/36wNNMb**.

In pairs or groups of three, **discuss** the following:

1 Why are the elements described in the table on the left important for theatre performances?
2 Who do the stage directions benefit the most?
3 How might asides help us learn more about characters?
4 Find some **images of stage sets for some of Shakespeare's plays**. How might a set influence the audience's reaction to the play?

How can Shakespeare's plays teach us about people and society?

HOW ARE WOMEN PRESENTED IN SHAKESPEARE'S PLAYS?

■ Elizabeth I was Queen of England and Ireland from 1558 until her death in 1603

■ Juliet and Cleopatra – not so different after all

Despite there being a queen on the throne, life for women in England during Shakespeare's time wasn't great. Women were dependent on their male relatives for financial support – in fact, they were seen almost as *belonging* to their fathers, brothers and eventually their husbands.

Unless they were widows, women didn't have the right to own any property of their own, which might explain why Queen Elizabeth decided not to marry. Speaking of marriage, if you were a girl and from a relatively wealthy family, you *could* potentially be married off at the ripe old age of … twelve!

The literature of the period often reflected society's attitudes towards women. The role of women in society at the time was very limited and women were expected to behave in a particular way. Because of this, in many Elizabethan and Jacobean plays, the female characters were often two dimensional and lacked any real depth.

Women, more often than not, fell into two categories: those who dared to challenge existing norms were presented as 'unnatural' villains, while those who conformed were celebrated as heroines or depicted as victims.

Shakespeare's women, however, don't always fit neatly into these categories and their roles can be difficult to judge. Let's take Juliet and Cleopatra, for example. At first glance they seem totally different. Juliet seems to be the ideal woman (according to standards at the time) – she is beautiful, kind and submissive; Cleopatra on the other hand is powerful, ambitious and defiant – all highly undesirable traits to a Shakespearean audience. But dig deeper, and you'll find that they aren't so different after all: Juliet stands up to her father for the sake of her love for Romeo, and Cleopatra is hopelessly devoted to her lover Mark Antony.

■ Wealthy women wore very elaborate clothing during Shakespeare's time. These garments were restrictive, fussy and even damaging to their health

Did you know ...

... that during Shakespeare's lifetime women were not permitted to perform on stage? You may wonder how this would have worked, considering there are well over a hundred female characters in his 38 plays. Well, the female parts were played by men.

Shakespeare's women are far from simple – they are complex and their words and actions give us an insight into the inner and outer lives of women living in the sixteenth and seventeenth centuries.

Shakespeare's subjects translate incredibly well onto canvas and over the centuries, scenes and characters from his plays have inspired hundreds of works of art. Below, you can see two very famous examples.

Look at the two paintings. The first, by John Singer Sargent, is of the nineteenth-century actress Ellen Terry as Lady Macbeth from the play *Macbeth*. The one on the right is by John Everett Millais and shows the death of Ophelia in *Hamlet*.

ACTIVITY: Shakespeare's women

ATL

■ Collaboration skills: Listen actively to other perspectives and ideas

1 **In pairs or groups of three, look at the paintings and match the adjectives below to the women depicted in the paintings.**

beautiful	majestic	melancholy	powerful
submissive	sad	strong	triumphant
virtuous	vulnerable	weak	wicked

2 **Discuss what you think each word means and justify your choices.**

◆ Assessment opportunities

◆ In this activity you have practised skills that are assessed using Criterion B: Organizing.

■ *Ellen Terry as Lady Macbeth* by John Singer Sargent

■ *Ophelia* by John Everett Millais

ACTIVITY: Wonder women

■ **ATL**

■ Communication skills:
  Make inferences and
  draw conclusions

1 **Read the brief descriptions
  of some of Shakespeare's
  most memorable female
  creations and, in pairs or
  groups of three, decide
  which IB learner profile
  attributes each possesses.**

2 **Each description is
  accompanied by a quote
  from the character. Discuss
  this and make notes on the
  language and stylistic choices
  made by Shakespeare.**

3 **Now, choose one of the
  characters you have
  discussed and write a
  paragraph explaining
  which IB learner profile
  attributes they possess. Use
  evidence from the quote
  provided to support and
  justify your response.**

◆ Assessment
  opportunities

◆ In this activity you have
  practised skills that are
  assessed using Criterion A:
  Analysing and Criterion D:
  Using language.

Name: Portia

Play: *The Merchant of Venice*

Best known for: Outwitting Shylock and saving Antonio's life.

In the play, Antonio, a merchant, binds himself to a rather grisly contract with the money lender Shylock, to allow his friend Bassanio (who happens to be Portia's love interest) to borrow three thousand ducats. Antonio is unable to pay back Shylock's money and as a result, is required to give him a pound of his flesh in return.

Luckily for Antonio, Portia disguises herself as a lawyer's apprentice and saves the day. Portia uses the exact language used in the contract to undermine Shylock's claim on Antonio's bond – after all, the contract states only 'a pound of flesh' can be extracted with no mention of the blood that is likely to be spilt. Clever!

'Tarry a little. There is something else.
This bond doth give thee here no jot of blood.
The words expressly are 'a pound of flesh.'
Take then thy bond, take thou thy pound of flesh,
But in the cutting it if thou dost shed
One drop of Christian blood, thy lands and goods
Are by the laws of Venice confiscate
Unto the state of Venice.'

If you want people to think you know what you're talking about, throw in some subject-specific language. Find some examples to show us why you would rely on Portia to represent you in court.

Name: Desdemona

Play: *Othello*

Best known for: Challenging social convention for the sake of love.

Today, we celebrate diversity and recognize that people shouldn't be discriminated against because of their ethnicity, religion, disability or class. People in Shakespeare's society, however, weren't as tolerant when it came to racial difference. Shakespeare boldly explores these themes in *Othello*.

In the play, Desdemona, a white Venetian woman, marries the noble general Othello, who is likely to be of North African descent, much to the disapproval of her father and other members of her community. Desdemona fearlessly stands by her decision, claiming that her love for Othello is beyond social and racial boundaries.

'That I did love the Moor to live with him,
My downright violence and storm of fortunes
May trumpet to the world. My heart's subdued
Even to the very quality of my lord.
I saw Othello's visage in his mind,
And to his honour and his valiant parts
Did I my soul and fortunes consecrate.'

There's a great message here – we should value personality over appearance. Can you find the line that sums this up perfectly?

Name: Viola

Play: *Twelfth Night*

Best known for: Acting as a go-between for Orsino and Olivia.

In the play, Viola and her twin brother Sebastian are separated during a shipwreck. Viola finds herself stranded in Illyria and disguises herself as a boy to enter the service of Orsino, a Duke who is desperately in love with a lady of noble birth called Olivia.

Viola, or Cesario as she is known, is employed to carry messages from the Duke to his beloved, but is so eloquent that Olivia ends up falling in love with her instead of Orsino.

'Most radiant, exquisite and unmatchable beauty, – I pray you, tell me if this be the lady of the house, for I never saw her: I would be loath to cast away my speech, for besides that it is excellently well penned, I have taken great pains to con it. Good beauties, let me sustain no scorn; I am very compatible, even to the least sinister usage.'

Who doesn't love a compliment? What language does Viola use to flatter Olivia?

Name: Queen Margaret

Play: *Henry VI, parts i, ii* and *iii; Richard III*

Best known for: Her bravery in battle.

Based on a real historical figure, Queen Margaret arrives in England from France to find that her husband, King Henry VI, is a weak and sickly man, too easily inclined to trust in the goodness of others who don't always have his interests at heart. Margaret begins to take over for him and proves herself to be powerful in the court.

When the future of her son as king appears to be in danger, she leads armies into battle against her enemies. Because of her ruthless approach and appetite for power, Margaret is disliked by the men around her as they believe her behaviour 'unnatural' and not that expected of women at the time.

'Seems he a dove? his feathers are but borrowed,
For he's disposed as the hateful raven:
Is he a lamb? his skin is surely lent him,
For he's inclined as is the ravenous wolf.
Who cannot steal a shape that means deceit?
Take heed, my lord; the welfare of us all
Hangs on the cutting short that fraudful man.'

There's some great animal **imagery** here. Why does Margaret use these comparisons?

King Lear and Cordelia. *Shakespeare*.

Name: Cordelia

Play: *King Lear*

Best known for: Being banished from the kingdom by her father for daring to be honest.

At the start of the play, Lear is deciding how best to divide his kingdom between the three of his daughters. To help him decide, he asks each of them to tell him how much they love him. His two eldest daughters, Goneril and Regan, make elaborate speeches, exaggerating their love and flattering their father. Cordelia, however, cannot find the words to express her love and expresses her feelings for her father with simplicity.

She stands by her beliefs and refuses to betray her true nature for the sake of material gain. Her father is angered by her reserve and as a result she is sent into exile.

'Good my lord,
You have begot me, bred me, loved me. I
Return those duties back as are right fit –
Obey you, love you, and most honour you.
Why have my sisters husbands if they say
They love you all? Haply when I shall wed
That lord whose hand must take my plight shall carry
Half my love with him, half my care and duty.
Sure, I shall never marry like my sisters,
To love my father all.'

What a sensible girl. What does the language Cordelia uses show us about her character and what she values most? How do we know she thinks carefully about things?

Why are there so many speeches in Shakespeare's plays?

Shakespeare loved a good speech and his plays are absolutely full of them. Speeches are a powerful tool, which we can use to communicate our ideas on issues we feel passionate about. They allow us to address a number of people at once and give us the opportunity to play with language to achieve a desired result.

Some of the speeches delivered by the characters in Shakespeare's plays give us a glimpse into the minds of those characters and help to create a sense of intimacy between them and the audience. As audience members, speeches can make us feel engaged, involved and sometimes even powerful.

In Shakespearean drama, speeches fall into two main categories: **soliloquies** and **monologues**.

In a soliloquy a character speaks their thoughts aloud, usually (but not always) when they are alone; the word itself comes from Latin, and means 'talking by oneself'.

Sometimes characters deliver soliloquies while there are other characters on stage, but it is generally accepted that their words cannot be heard by anyone other than the audience. This allows characters to communicate their thoughts, feelings or intentions directly to the audience.

Soliloquies are carefully crafted to create strong feelings in the audience about specific characters; as the audience is led deeper into the mind of a character, they can experience anything from feelings of pity to sheer horror.

A monologue on the other hand, is an uninterrupted speech that characters make to other characters in the play. Monologues (much like soliloquies) are sometimes used by characters to express their feelings or explain their intentions.

These speeches, especially when addressed to a larger group of people or a crowd, can be used to convince other characters to think or feel a certain way about something.

In this section, we will take a closer look at some of the most famous speeches in the plays of William Shakespeare.

A step-by-step guide to writing speeches

A speech is a formal address delivered to an audience. The speaker, or **orator**, usually has a very specific purpose in mind and most speeches are persuasive.

Persuasive communication is also known as **rhetoric** and in order to achieve the desired purpose, the writer or speaker has to make specific stylistic choices.

The prospect of writing a speech for the first time can be quite daunting, so here's a step-by-step guide to get you started:

1 **Begin with a brief welcome or greeting.** Your audience is incredibly important and if you want to change their mind or get them on your side, it's a good idea to use direct address to get them involved. First impressions are everything, so spend time crafting your opening line.

2 **Outline what you are going to talk about.** Make sure your audience knows what your purpose is. Be clear and concise – you don't want them to get lost.

3 **Make three or four key points (one per paragraph).** Make sure you present your ideas in a logical order. Later, we'll look in more depth at ways in which you can keep your audience gripped.

4 **End with something memorable or interesting.** Now that you've presented your ideas, you don't want your audience to wander off and forget what you said. Think carefully about your final words … and don't forget to acknowledge the audience once more at the end.

So, you've got the basics down. Now let's see how you can enrich your writing with some **rhetorical** techniques. And who best to help us? William Shakespeare, of course.

In the speech from *Julius Caesar,* on page 140, Mark Antony stands before Rome to deliver a funeral speech about his beloved friend and emperor, Julius Caesar, who has just been brutally murdered by Brutus and some other conspirators.

ACTIVITY: The art of rhetoric

ATL

- Communication skills: Read critically and for comprehension

Read the speech on page 140.

1 Using what you have just learnt about writing speeches, **evaluate** the structure of Mark Antony's speech.

2 **Consider** all of the stylistic devices identified in the speech. How do they help to make the speech more persuasive? What is the effect of each device?

3 Now watch the short clip from the 1953 film adaptation of *Julius Caesar,* and listen to Marlon Brando performing the speech: **https://youtu.be/7X9C55TkUP8.**

    Which words in particular does Brando stress or emphasize? When does he raise or lower the volume of his voice? **Discuss** how these differences can affect the meaning of his words and the impact they may have on the audience.

◆ Assessment opportunities

- In this activity you have practised skills that are assessed using Criterion A: Analysing.

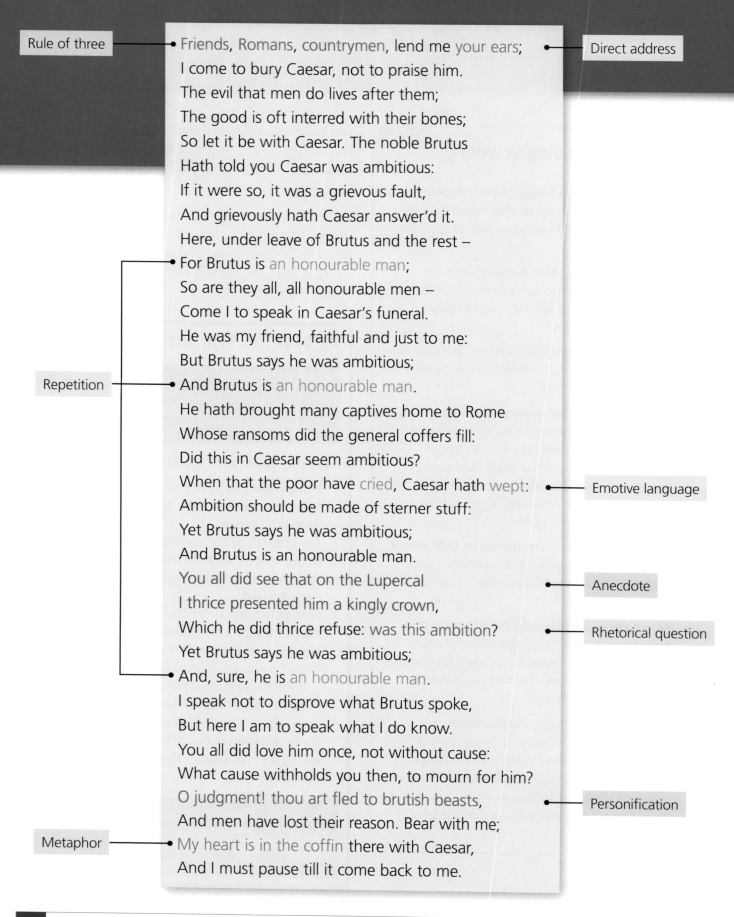

Rule of three • Friends, Romans, countrymen, lend me your ears; • Direct address
I come to bury Caesar, not to praise him.
The evil that men do lives after them;
The good is oft interred with their bones;
So let it be with Caesar. The noble Brutus
Hath told you Caesar was ambitious:
If it were so, it was a grievous fault,
And grievously hath Caesar answer'd it.
Here, under leave of Brutus and the rest –
For Brutus is an honourable man;
So are they all, all honourable men –
Come I to speak in Caesar's funeral.
He was my friend, faithful and just to me:
But Brutus says he was ambitious;
Repetition • And Brutus is an honourable man.
He hath brought many captives home to Rome
Whose ransoms did the general coffers fill:
Did this in Caesar seem ambitious?
When that the poor have cried, Caesar hath wept: • Emotive language
Ambition should be made of sterner stuff:
Yet Brutus says he was ambitious;
And Brutus is an honourable man.
You all did see that on the Lupercal • Anecdote
I thrice presented him a kingly crown,
Which he did thrice refuse: was this ambition? • Rhetorical question
Yet Brutus says he was ambitious;
And, sure, he is an honourable man.
I speak not to disprove what Brutus spoke,
But here I am to speak what I do know.
You all did love him once, not without cause:
What cause withholds you then, to mourn for him?
O judgment! thou art fled to brutish beasts, • Personification
And men have lost their reason. Bear with me;
Metaphor • My heart is in the coffin there with Caesar,
And I must pause till it come back to me.

To be, or not to be – that is the question:
Whether 'tis nobler in the mind to suffer
The slings and arrows of outrageous fortune,
Or to take arms against a sea of troubles,
And by opposing end them? To die: – to sleep –
No more; and by a sleep to say we end
The heartache and the thousand natural shocks
That flesh is heir to, 'tis a consummation
Devoutly to be wish'd. To die, to sleep;
To sleep: perchance to dream: ay, there's the rub;
For in that sleep of death what dreams may come
When we have shuffled off this mortal coil,
Must give us pause: there's the respect
That makes calamity of so long life;
For who would bear the whips and scorns of time,
The oppressor's wrong, the proud man's contumely,
The pangs of despised love, the law's delay,
The insolence of office and the spurns
That patient merit of the unworthy takes,
When he himself might his quietus make
With a bare bodkin? who would fardels bear,
To grunt and sweat under a weary life,
But that the dread of something after death,
The undiscover'd country from whose bourn
No traveller returns, puzzles the will
And makes us rather bear those ills we have
Than fly to others that we know not of?
Thus conscience does make cowards of us all;
And thus the native hue of resolution
Is sicklied o'er with the pale cast of thought,
And enterprises of great pitch and moment
With this regard their currents turn awry,
And lose the name of action.

Isn't it ironic?

You may have noticed that in his speech Mark Antony repeats one phrase in particular – *'And Brutus is an honourable man.'* But does he really mean what he says? Does he truly believe that Brutus is 'honourable'?

The answer is no. He means exactly the opposite of what he says. This is what is known as **irony**, and by repeating this again and again, he makes this clear to the audience.

We come across irony not just in literature but also in everyday situations. Think back to a time when you might have said something that is the opposite of what you truly felt at a particular moment – like looking out of the window on a rainy day and remarking, 'Lovely, isn't it?'

In drama we also come across another form of irony – **dramatic irony**. This is when you as an audience member or reader know more than the characters in the play. Many filmmakers make use of dramatic irony to create suspense and to keep viewers engaged. Seeing dramatic irony in action can be incredibly frustrating and nerve wracking – especially, for example, in horror movies when you, the viewer, watches helplessly as a group of unsuspecting teenagers walk into a creepy, dilapidated building where you *know* horrors await them.

ACTIVITY: To be or not to be …

■ ATL

- Media literacy skills: Demonstrate awareness of media interpretations of events and ideas

Quite possibly the most quoted phrase in literature, 'to be or not to be' has made the **eponymous protagonist** of *Hamlet* an **icon** of Shakespearean drama. Hamlet's famous soliloquy has been read, performed, misunderstood, interpreted and reinterpreted countless times since its debut in the early seventeenth century.

Watch the following clips from three different film versions of *Hamlet*. Copy and complete the table below, adding notes about the way in which the speech has been performed.

You can find the clips by typing the following search terms in a search engine: **to be or not to be** followed by **Hawke** then **Olivier** and finally **Brannagh**.

The speech appears on page 141 so you can read along if you like.

Version	Setting	Props and costumes	Mood or tone
Ethan Hawke			
Lawrence Olivier			
Kenneth Brannagh			

Now, in pairs or groups of three, use your table to **discuss** the following:

1 **Compare and contrast** the three interpretations. What similarities and differences can you **identify**?
2 Which version do you think would appeal most to a modern-day audience? Consider how the setting, props and costumes might have an impact.
3 Which version do you think best captures the mood or tone of the speech?
4 Did you understand what the speech is about? What is Hamlet's dilemma?
5 Look back at the contexts handbook you made earlier (see page 129). How does Hamlet's soliloquy reflect the religious beliefs of the sixteenth century?

◆ Assessment opportunities

◆ In this activity you have practised skills that are assessed using Criterion A: Analysing.

ⓘ No Fear Shakespeare

Still finding it hard to make head or tail of Shakespeare? Well, have no fear!

No Fear Shakespeare is a wonderful online resource which places the original text of Shakespeare's plays alongside a modern version.

Find the modern version of Hamlet's soliloquy here: **https://bit.ly/3jdu4qi**.

There is also a selection of animated summaries of some of Shakespeare's plays, so take a look around.

EXTENSION: SHAKESPEARE SOLOS

The year 2016 saw the 400th anniversary of Shakespeare's death. To mark the occasion, the *Guardian* newspaper invited leading actors to perform some of the playwright's greatest speeches: **https://bit.ly/3ol0zha**.

Think you could do better? Find the text of some of your favourite Shakespearean speeches and have a go yourself.

If, like Caesar, you're feeling particularly ambitious, try to learn at least one speech off by heart. Don't worry if you don't understand every word – for this task it's the performance that matters.

Ask your peers to test how well you've done.

Are the themes explored in Shakespeare's plays as relevant today as they were in his day?

Four hundred years have passed since Shakespeare's death and his plays are as popular as ever. We cannot deny the power of his writing and must recognize the impact it has had on our culture, language and imagination. But is Shakespeare's work still relevant in our world today? The answer is yes.

The timeless appeal of Shakespeare's writing lies not just in his eloquent verse. It is his compelling plots and his exploration of themes such as love, death, betrayal and ambition which shed light on the human experience, that have captured the interest of audiences for centuries. Through the behaviour of his complex and varied characters we develop a deeper understanding of human nature.

In plays such as *The Merchant of Venice* and *Othello*, we learn important lessons about the dangers of ugly behaviour and prejudice, whether based on ethnicity, religion or social class – issues that we still battle with in our lives today.

■ What do all of the above have in common? They're all from adaptations of Shakespeare's plays. *10 Things I Hate About You* is an adaptation of *The Taming of the Shrew*, while *She's the Man* is based on *Twelfth Night*; *The Lion King* is inspired by *Hamlet*, and *Gnomeo & Juliet* … Well, you can probably figure out that one for yourself.

In the world of literature, Shakespeare isn't just important – he is necessary. Although some of his plots may not be entirely original (he might have 'borrowed' from other stories), his plays have influenced and inspired generations of writers and will continue to do so for years to come.

Shakespeare's plays have crossed the boundaries not only of time but also space. His work is widely read across the globe. People from all backgrounds can find something in his plays to which they can relate, and this love and shared appreciation of his work can help us make meaningful connections with others.

SHAKESPEARE ON SCREEN

Not everyone is as enthusiastic about Shakespeare's work as you might think. Some people find his plays difficult to understand because of the language. When students are first introduced to Shakespeare in the classroom, they can find his fussy phrases and complicated plots rather daunting. So, how can we get over this? Well, cinema might be the answer.

Shakespeare's plays were a huge hit with audiences in his time – and not much has changed today. The film industry realized the potential of his plays and scriptwriters began to adapt his work for the big screen. The first Shakespeare film dates back to 1899. Many of these films used the language of his original plays but others are looser adaptations and are aimed at modern audiences.

An adaptation is the transfer of a written text to film. Key parts of the text, such as the basic plot and characters remain the same, but the language may be changed and not all of the text is always used.

Here's an excerpt from the script for *She's the Man* (left) where Viola asks her friend Paul to help transform her into a boy; and an extract from Act I, scene ii of *Twelfth Night* (right) where Viola seeks help from the captain of their ship following the wreck.

Paul: You want me to turn you into your brother?

Viola: That's right. I'm going to Illyria as Sebastian. I'll make the boys' soccer team, and in 12 days beat the Cornwall boys' team.

Paul: You've taken too many soccer balls to the head.

Viola: You know I can do it, Paul.

Paul: Except for the voice, mannerisms, the breasts, the mentality and …

Friend 1: It doesn't matter. Nobody at Illyria has even met Sebastian.

Girl 1: They won't know the difference.

Paul: They'll know he's a girl.

Viola: Oh, come on, Paul.

Viola and friends: Yeah, come on, Paul.

Woman at Salon: Yeah, come on, Paul.

Paul: OK. OK. I'll see what I can do.

Viola and friends: Yes!

VIOLA: There is a fair behaviour in thee, captain,
And though that nature with a beauteous wall
Doth oft close in pollution, yet of thee
I will believe thou hast a mind that suits
With this thy fair and outward character.
I prithee – and I'll pay thee bounteously –
Conceal me what I am, and be my aid
For such disguise as haply shall become
The form of my intent. I'll serve this duke.
Thou shall present me as an eunuch to him.
It may be worth thy pains, for I can sing
And speak to him in many sorts of music
That will allow me very worth his service.
What else may hap to time I will commit.
Only shape thou thy silence to my wit.

ACTIVITY: Shakespeare on screen

ATL

- Information literacy skills: Use critical-literacy skills to analyse and interpret media communications
- Critical-thinking skills: Gather and organize relevant information to formulate an argument

1 After watching a trailer for *She's the Man*, complete the following tasks. In pairs or groups of three, **discuss**:

- Are you surprised that this film is based on a play by Shakespeare? **Explain** why.
- Is this a film you would be interested in watching? Why? Which parts in particular appeal to you?
- What is the effect of changing the setting to a modern-day one? Why do you think the creators decided to set the play in a high school?
- Which modern-day issues faced by teenagers do you think the film addresses? What does this reveal to us about Shakespeare's plays?
- Do you think it's acceptable to change the language of Shakespeare's plays to suit modern audiences?

2 Now **compare** the two extracts on page 145.

- What do both of the Violas have in common?
- What motivates each girl to do what she wants to do?
- What does this show us about the societies the girls live in? Have things changed a great deal since Shakespeare's time?
- How does each character persuade other characters to help them achieve what they want? In your opinion, whose language is most effective?

◆ Assessment opportunities

- ◆ In this activity you have practised skills that are assessed using Criterion A: Analysing and Criterion D: Using language.

■ In 2012, the Globe Theatre in London staged 37 of Shakespeare's plays in 37 different languages as part of their *Globe to Globe* festival. Here you can see the Ngakau Toa group from New Zealand performing *Troilus and Cressida* in Maori (top) and the Roy-e-Sabs theatre company from Afghanistan acting out a scene from *A Comedy of Errors* in Persian. Find out more about some of the other Shakespeare plays performed in other languages here: **https://bit.ly/3pTFm5e**.

Is something lost in translation when we perform Shakespeare in other languages?

Does Shakespeare belong to the world? Why, of course. To limit his work to the English-speaking world would be plain selfish. Thankfully, Shakespeare's plays have been translated into more than 80 languages and adapted for both stage and film across the world. It was in 1741 that one of Shakespeare's plays was translated into another language for the first time – the play was *Julius Caesar* and the language German, in case you were wondering.

But is 'Shakespeare' Shakespeare if it isn't performed in Shakespeare's English? Is there something lost in translation, and if so, does this matter?

Let's hear what the experts think. Listen to this podcast 'Shakespeare in Translation' from the Folger Shakespeare Library: **https://bit.ly/3tndoRU**.

(You only need to listen to the first eight minutes.)

ACTIVITY: Around the world in 80 languages

■ ATL

- Critical-thinking skills: Evaluate evidence and arguments

After you have listened to the podcast, in pairs or groups of three, **discuss** these questions:

1 **What is the most important thing about Shakespeare's writing? Is it a compelling story, compelling characters or beautiful poetic language?**
2 **According to some scholars, what problems do we come across when we translate Shakespeare's plays?**
3 **Is it important that Shakespeare's plays contain Shakespeare's language?**
4 **Is there anything at all that can be preserved in the translation of his plays?**
5 **What matters most: the language or the story?**
6 **Have you ever seen a production of a play by Shakespeare in a language other than English? Use a search engine to find some examples.**

Let's have a debate

In groups, note down some possible ideas for debate linked to the topic of Shakespeare in translation. Use the guidelines on page 148 about setting up a debate.

In order for a debate to be successful, you should make sure you know your stuff, so you need to start researching. Here's a useful website to help you get started:

https://bit.ly/2O0qswf

◆ Assessment opportunities

- In this activity you have practised skills that are assessed using Criterion B: Organizing and Criterion D: Using language.

Setting up a debate

How would you like to have a full-blown argument in your classroom *with* your teacher's approval? No chance? Think again. That's just what a debate is … well, sort of.

A debate allows you to argue about a subject in a formal manner. It's a great way to develop your critical thinking, communication, teamwork and research skills. *And* it can be a lot of fun.

Debates usually follow a fairly fixed structure and the participants should put their ideas across in a clear and logical manner. The point of a debate is to get other people to accept your point of view and, as you have seen already in this chapter, persuasion takes a lot of skill.

To find out more about how to set up a successful debate, visit the websites below and make some notes.

- https://youtu.be/EDTk-_Lt6sQ
- https://bit.ly/2YFhfLI

Hints and tips

- Always be yourself.
- You must appear confident.
- Listen to questions or points raised by other speakers.
- Think about the audience's attention span. You don't want them to drop off to sleep.
- Make your answers and points relevant. Be concise.
- Know your material. (That's where your research comes in.)
- Write down any important names or information. This will make you feel less anxious.

debate an exchange in which two opposing teams make speeches to support their arguments and disagree with those of the other team

motion a formal proposal for debate, which is put to the vote

opposition the team opposed to the motion

proposition the team in favour of the motion

persuade to convince another person or team to do something or adopt a point of view by argument or reasoning

argument a fact or statement put forward as proof or evidence

resolution the opinion about which two teams argue

affirmative team agrees with the resolution

negative team disagrees with the resolution

rebuttal explains why one team disagrees with the other team

judges/audience decide the winner

A basic structure for the debate

At the start of the debate, each team introduces their main line of argument in a three-minute speech.

1 The chairperson introduces the topic and the proposition and opposition teams.

2 Each team introduces their main line of argument in a three-minute speech.

3 The first **proposition speaker** gives a **full overview** of the topic and their view.

4 The first **opposition speaker** offers a **rebuttal** against what the first proposition speaker has said and comes up with a **new argument**.

5 The second **proposition speaker** responds and gives their view along with any new points.

6 The second **opposition speaker** gives their speech.

7 The third **proposition speaker** responds and gives their view along with any new points.

8 The third **opposition speaker** gives their speech.

9 The debate is **opened to the floor**.

10 The **opposition speaker makes closing comments and summarizes** the opposition's arguments.

11 The **proposition speaker makes closing comments and summarizes** their main arguments.

12 The floor votes.

To add more depth to your speeches, refer back to Mark Antony's speech on page 140. See if you can make your arguments more persuasive by including some rhetorical techniques.

◆ Assessment opportunities

◆ In this activity you have practised skills that are assessed using Criterion A: Analysing, Criterion B: Organizing and Criterion D: Using language.

! Take action: How can I make a difference?

! We could all do with more Shakespeare in our lives. People can be put off by the difficult language in his plays, but once you get over that, you'll learn that Shakespeare can be great fun. Here are some things you can do:

◆ **See a play:** You might need your parents to help with this one. Shakespeare's plays are *always* on somewhere. Keep an eye out for performances at theatres near you and go and see one. It might be hard to keep up with the dialogue at first, but you can always sneak a peek at a summary online before you go. If you can't find a theatre production, then watch a film version instead.

◆ **Stage your own production:** Ever wanted to be a director? Or perhaps you're an actor in the making. Get together with some friends and perform one of Shakespeare's plays for your next school assembly. We recommend a light-hearted comedy. Ask your Drama teacher to help you organize your play.

◆ **Make a modern-day film adaptation:** Like the sound of the story from one of Shakespeare's plays but think it could do with a bit of an update? Try your hand at planning a modern-day film adaptation of one of Shakespeare's plays. Make a storyboard to prepare for filming. Think carefully about locations and props. You could try to film a scene from your film.

SOME SUMMATIVE TASKS TO TRY

Use these tasks to apply and extend your learning in this chapter. These tasks are designed so that you can evaluate your learning at different levels of achievement in the Language and literature criteria.

THIS TASK CAN BE USED TO EVALUATE YOUR LEARNING IN CRITERION B, CRITERION C AND CRITERION D

Task 1: Sympathy for Shylock

Read Shylock's speech from Act III, scene i of *The Merchant of Venice* (right). Here Shylock, a Jew, who feels discriminated against by those around him simply because he is of a different faith, passionately explains why he insists on taking a pound of flesh from Antonio.

Explain how Shakespeare uses language and stylistic devices to create sympathy for Shylock. Make sure you quote from the text to support and **justify** your explanation.

Aim to write at least four PEA paragraphs.

Task 2: To read Shakespeare, or not to read Shakespeare …

Think back to what you have learnt so far in this chapter about speeches and review what you now know about Shakespeare and his work.

Write a speech for your classmates to convince them that they should be more enthusiastic about studying Shakespeare at school.

Make sure you think carefully about your use of language and that you include rhetorical devices.

> To bait fish withal: if it will feed nothing else, it will feed my revenge. He hath disgraced me, and hindered me half a million; laughed at my losses, mocked at my gains, scorned my nation, thwarted my bargains, cooled my friends, heated mine enemies; and what's his reason? I am a Jew. Hath not a Jew eyes? hath not a Jew hands, organs, dimensions, senses, affections, passions? fed with the same food, hurt with the same weapons, subject to the same diseases, healed by the same means, warmed and cooled by the same winter and summer, as a Christian is? If you prick us, do we not bleed? if you tickle us, do we not laugh? if you poison us, do we not die? and if you wrong us, shall we not revenge? If we are like you in the rest, we will resemble you in that. If a Jew wrong a Christian, what is his humility? Revenge. If a Christian wrong a Jew, what should his sufferance be by Christian example? Why, revenge. The villany you teach me, I will execute, and it shall go hard but I will better the instruction.

Reflection

In this chapter we have explored the life and work of William Shakespeare and developed an understanding of the **conventions** of drama and some forms of poetry. As part of this process, we have developed an understanding of how Shakespeare uses **language** and makes **stylistic choices** to weave elaborate storylines and create rich and convincing characters. In addition, we have considered Shakespeare's work as being an essential part of our literary and cultural heritage and have celebrated the power of his writing to break through the barriers of space and time.

Use this table to reflect on your own learning in this chapter.					
Questions we asked	Answers we found	Any further questions now?			
Factual: Who was William Shakespeare? Was Shakespeare a poet or a playwright? What is a sonnet? What is a play?					
Conceptual: How can Shakespeare's plays teach us about people and society? How are women presented in Shakespeare's plays? Why are there so many speeches in Shakespeare's plays?					
Debatable: Are the themes explored in Shakespeare's plays as relevant today as when they were written? Is something lost in translation when we perform Shakespeare in other languages?					
Approaches to learning you used in this chapter:	Description – what new skills did you learn?	How well did you master the skills?			
		Novice	Learner	Practitioner	Expert
Collaboration skills					
Communication skills					
Creative-thinking skills					
Critical-thinking skills					
Information literacy skills					
Media literacy skills					
Learner profile attribute(s)	Reflect on the importance of being an inquirer for your learning in this chapter.				
Inquirer					

Glossary

act One of the main divisions of a play

alliteration The repetition of sounds in a sentence or a line

alternate rhyme ABAB rhyme scheme; the alternation of two different rhymes in a sequence of four or more lines

annotation Notes or comments that you make about a text (or image) while reading it

audience imperative Refers to the impact a text has on an intended audience

blurb A short description of a book or a film

caption A brief explanation or comment accompanying an image

characterization Describing the characteristics or qualities of a character in a text; used to make them appear more realistic

colloquial language Everyday language and expressions as used in conversation

connotation The associations that a word or image has; implied meanings

contemporary realism or **realistic fiction** Tries to create characters that you could imagine living in the real world

context Something that affects the meaning outside of the text, such as its time period or country

conventions The features of language that describe how language works and enables us to use it accurately

couplet A pair of successive lines of verse, typically rhyming and of the same length

denotation The actual meaning of a word or phrase; what an image actually shows us

dialogue A conversation between two or more people; what is said by the characters in a story, film or play

direct address Using personal pronouns to directly involve the audience

dramatic irony When the audience members or readers know more than the characters in a play or film

dramatis personae A list of the characters in a play

ekphrastic poem A poem based on or describing a scene depicted in a painting

emotive language Language that evokes an emotional response from the reader and can influence the tone or mood of a text

eponymous protagonist This is when the title of a story is given the same name as the main character or protagonist. For example, Othello is the title of play but also the name of the main character – he is therefore the eponymous protagonist

exposition A literary device that presents essential information about events, settings and characters to an audience. Without exposition, a story would be difficult to follow

expository genre See **exposition**

figurative language Uses **similes**, **metaphors**, **hyperbole** and **personification** to describe something, often by comparing it with something else

first conditional Used to talk about things that are likely to happen in the future, based on a possible action in the present

first person pronoun I (singular), we (plural)

flashback A part of a story or film that describes or shows something that happened in the past

foreshadowing Where a writer hints at what is to come later on in the text

genre A style of text or film

hyperbole Extreme exaggeration used to enhance the effect of a statement

iambic pentameter A line of verse with five metrical feet, each consisting of one unstressed syllable followed by one stressed syllable

icon A person or thing which represents or symbolizes something, for example, Marylin Monroe was a Hollywood icon in the 1950s

imagery Very descriptive words that build an image, or picture, in the reader's mind

imperative Verbs or sentences that are used to give commands or instructions

impressionistic language Language used to create an initial idea, feeling or opinion about something or someone

inclusive pronouns we, us

irony Use of words to give a meaning that is different from its literal meaning

literal language Language that means exactly what it says

metaphor A literary technique which allows us to say that a person, place, animal or thing *is* something else, rather than just similar to it

monologue An uninterrupted speech that characters make to other characters in the play

motif A recurring idea or image in a story

narrative A story or account of events

omniscient A narrator that has knowledge of all times, people, places and events, and all characters' thoughts

onomatopoeia Words that sound like their meaning, for example: crash, bang

orator A public speaker

over the shoulder narrative When the narrator knows only as much as the characters and describes the events as they unfold

personification A literary technique used to give inanimate objects or concepts human characteristics

perspective The author's point of view within a text

playwright A writer of plays

presentational devices Features that are used in addition to the writing in a text

primary source A source of information that was created by a person during a particular period in history

prose Written or spoken language presented in an ordinary way

purpose The writer's reason for writing

quatrain A four-line stanza

realistic fiction Stories that resemble real life and take place in believable settings

Received Pronunciation (RP) A way of speaking English that is sometimes described as 'very British' and is easily identified

register The style and use of language used in a specific context

repetition Words or phrases that are repeated for effect

rhetoric Persuasive speaking or writing

rhyme A rhyme is a repetition of similar sounding words occurring usually at the end of lines in a poem or song

rhythm The beat of a poem

rule of three A list of three words of the same word class, used for emphasis and effect

scene A division of an act in a play during which the action takes place in a single place without a break in time

second person pronoun you (singular and plural)

secondary source Information that is created by someone else who is studying a particular historical period

sibilance The repetition of sibilant sounds (s, sh, z) for effect

simile A way of describing something by comparing it to something else, often using the word 'like' or 'as'

slang The opposite of Standard English; language that is used informally, particularly in speaking

soliloquy Where a character speaks their thoughts aloud, usually (but not always) when they are alone

sonnet A poem of fourteen lines with specific rhythm and rhyme

Standard English The style of English language in all its forms, writing and speaking, that is considered to be the accepted way to communicate, especially in a formal context

stock character Characters that traditionally represent stereotypes with which we are familiar

sub-genre A sub-division of a **genre** in literature or film

synonym A word that is the same in meaning as another word

tone The emotion or feelings that a text creates

tragic flaw A weakness possessed by a character in a story which is often the cause of their downfall; also known as a fatal flaw

trickster A character in a text who cheats or deceives people

verse Writing that is arranged with a rhythm; not prose

voice The person who is speaking in a text

volta The point at which the argument, idea or mood of a poem changes

Acknowledgements

The Publishers would like to thank the following for permission to reproduce copyright material. Every effort has been made to trace all copyright holders, but if any have been inadvertently overlooked the Publishers will be pleased to make the necessary arrangements at the first opportunity.

Photo credits

p.2 © Film Company Warner Bros/AF archive/Alamy Stock Photo; **p.4** *tl* © Inpix/Indiapicture/Alamy Stock Photo, *cl* © Stephen Simpson/Iconica/Getty Images; **p.5** © Interfoto/AKG Images; **p.6** © Kevin Britland/Alamy Stock Photo; **p.7** © Videologygroup.com; **p.10** © Number 9 Films/Ronald Grant Archive/Mary Evans; **p.14** *t* © Gainsborough/REX/Shutterstock, *c,b* © Everett Collection/REX/Shutterstock; **p.17** © Everett Collection/REX/Shutterstock, **p.18** © Associated Newspapers/REX/Shutterstock; **p.20** © Gina Kelly/Alamy Stock Photo; **p.22** *bl* © Snap Stills/REX/Shutterstock, *bc* © Paramount/Everett/REX/Shutterstock, *br* ©Fox Searchlight Pictures/Entertainment Pictures/ZUMA Press, Inc./Alamy Stock Photo; **p.24** © Hill Street Studios/Blend Images/Getty images; **p.25** © Brian Atkinson/Alamy Stock Photo; **p.26** © WANDYCZ Kasia/Paris Match Archive/Getty Images; **p.28** © Ancient Art & Architecture Collection Ltd/Alamy Stock Photo; **p.29** *tr* © Classic Image/Alamy Stock Photo, *tc* ©Film Company Marvel Studios/Walt Disney/AF archive/Alamy Stock Photo, *tl* © tsuneo/123RF; **p.33** © Photo Researchers, Inc/Alamy Stock Photo; **p.36** *t* © GL Archive/Alamy Stock Photo, *b* © Dinodia Photos/Alamy Stock Photo; **p.39** *t* © Sanjay Borra/Alamy Stock Photo, *br* © JLImages/Alamy Stock Photo, *bl* © Karl F. Schöfmann/imageBROKER/Alamy Stock Photo; **p.42** © Fine Art Images/Superstock; **p.44** © Ivy Close Images/Alamy Stock Photo; **p.50** © Film Company Fox 2000 Pictures/AF archive/Alamy Stock Photo; **p.53** © Tim Gainey/Alamy Stock Photo; **p.59** *tc* © Stanislav Istratov/123RF, *tl* © Elena Schweitzer/123RF, *tr* © shamain/123RF; **p.60** *tl* © Chris Hill/National Geographic/Getty Images, *tr* © wikimedia.org; **p.71** *t* © Geoffrey Swaine/REX/Shutterstock, *c* © Paul Quayle/Alamy Stock Photo, *b* © Adrian Sherratt/Alamy Stock Photo; **p.75** © Aloysius Patrimonio/123RF; **p.82** © Tony French/Alamy Stock Photo; **p.83** *tr* © Inge Johnsson/Alamy Stock Photo, *tl* © Ka Wing Yu/Alamy Stock Photo; **p.84** *bl* © Stephen Grant/Alamy Stock Photo, *br* © Jonathan Kingston/Aurora Photos/Alamy Stock Photo; **p.85** *bl* © Chris Batson/Alamy Stock Photo, *br* © Alistair Laming/Alamy Stock Photo; **p.87** © McDonald.com; **p.88** © Wateraid.org; **p.92** © ZUMA Press, Inc./Alamy Stock Photo; **p.94** © slena/123RF; **p.96** *b, tl* © The Advertising Archives/Alamy Stock Photo, *tr* © Hera Vintage Ads/Alamy Stock Photo; **p.97** *tl, tr* © The Advertising Archives/Alamy Stock Photo, *bl* © Hemis/Alamy Stock Photo; **p.98** *l, r* © The Advertising Archives/Alamy Stock Photo; **p.99** © The Granger Collection/TopFoto; **p.100** *l* © Blank Archives/Hulton Archive/GettyImages, *tr, br* © The Advertising Archives/Alamy Stock Photo; **p.101** © The Advertising Archives/Alamy Stock Photo; **p.104** © Lucian Coman/Fotolia; **p.106** © Federicofoto/123RF; **p.107** © Ginger Perry/AP/Press Association Images; **p.108** © Rob Kim/Stringer/Getty Images; **p.115** © RosaIreneBetancourt 9/Alamy Stock Photo; **p.117** © Tabatha Fireman/Redferns/GettyImages; **p.122** *tl* © INTERFOTO/Alamy Stock Photo, *tr* © ZUMA Press, Inc./Alamy Stock Photo; **p.126** *t* © Jeffrey Blackler/Alamy Stock Photo, *b* © DENIS SINYAKOV/AFP/Gettyimages; **p.127** ©June green/Alamy Stock Photo; **p.128** *t* © Archivart/Alamy Stock Photo, *b* © Lebrecht Music and Arts Photo Library/Alamy Stock Photo; **p.133** *tl* © The Print Collector/Alamy Stock Photo, *tc, b* © Lebrecht Music and Arts Photo Library/Alamy Stock Photo, *tr* © Collection Christophel/Alamy Stock Photo; **p.135** *l* © Ivy Close Images/Alamy Stock Photo, *r* © Ian G Dagnall/Alamy Stock Photo; **p.135** © The Granger Collection/TopFoto; **p.136** *l* © DeAgostini/Getty Images, *r* © Christie's Images Ltd./Superstock; **p.137** *l* © Mary Evans Picture Library, *r* © Lebrecht Music and Arts Photo Library/Alamy Stock Photo; **p.144** *t* © United Archives GmbH/Alamy Stock Photo, *tc* © Rob McEwan/Dreamworks SKG/REX/Shutterstock, *bc* © Pictorial Press Ltd/Alamy Stock Photo, *b* © Collection Christophel/Alamy Stock Photo; **p.146** *t* © Theatrepix/Alamy Stock Photo, *b* © Daniel Naupold/DPA/PA Images

t = top, *b* = bottom, *c* = centre, *l* = left, *r* = right